AB

SHROUDED SECRETS

Japan's War on
Mainland Australia
1942-1944

Also from Brassey's

SHROUDED SECRETS

Japan's War on
Mainland Australia
1942-1944

Richard Connaughton

BRASSEY'S
LONDON • WASHINGTON

First English edition 1994

UK editorial offices: 33 John Street, London WC1N 2AT
orders: Marston Book Services, PO Box 87, Oxford OX2 0DT

USA orders: Order Department, Macmillan Publishing Company,
201 West 103rd Street, Inidanapolis, IN 46290

Distributed in North America to booksellers and wholesalers by the
Macmillan Publishing Company, NY 10022

Richard Connaughton has asserted his moral right to be identified
as author of this work.

Library of Congress Cataloguing in Publication Data
available

British Library Cataloguing in Publication Data
A catalogue record for this book is
available from the British Library

ISBN – 1-85753-160-4 Hardback

Typesetting and page make-up by
TypeBright, Burton upon Trent

Printed and bound in Great Britain
by Bookcraft (Bath) Ltd.

**For
Michael and Emma**

Contents

List of Plates

21. All that remains of the camp: the entrance
22. Cairn marking the point of breakout
23. Ishidoro in the Japanese War Cemetery
24. Australian graves in the Commonwealth Section of the War
    Cemetery, Cowra
25. The 1944 battlefield today

(Note: *Plates credited AWM are reproduced by kind permission of the Australian War Memorial, Canberra. The figures in brackets are the AWM negative numbers. Plates credited ARGC are from photographs taken by ARG Connaughton).*

List of maps and sketches

(All drawn by André Effendi)

Introduction

On Thursday, 27 February 1992, speaking of events in 1942, Australian Prime Minister Paul Keating claimed that Britain had 'decided not to defend the Malayan Peninsula, not to worry about Singapore and not to give us our troops back to keep ourselves free from Japanese domination'. Most political commentators attributed his outburst to political opportunism in playing the nationalist card to rally support and build up his own popularity rating. Is it legitimate, however, to fabricate for crude political gain such patent untruths when the servicemen of both Britain and Australia suffered such a cruel fate at the hands of a barbaric enemy?

If Keating had said that British leadership was inept and had based its military strategy on false premises, there could be little argument. Australia's lack of preparedness in December 1941, however, did not come about as an immediate prelude to the war but had its origins in earlier times. Ironically, a partial villain of the piece was Australia's Irish-Catholic dominated Labor Party (the Australian Labor Party adopted the American spelling of Labour in the 1890s), of which Paul Keating is a chip off the same block. In the 1930s, the Labor Party consistently opposed the expansion of Australia's Defence Forces. What Mr. Keating has done has been to emphasise the divide in Australian society; on the one hand the pro-British motherland element, as epitomised by the Liberal Party's Sir Robert Menzies and, on the other, an expanding republican movement with its roots firmly embedded in the mythology of the 1854 Eureka Stockade rebellion and now drawing strength from new world immigration. The Keating attack is reminiscent of the anti-British sentiments expounded by those of Irish Nationalist extraction in the 1920s-30s, one particular leader being J T (Jack) Lang. Lang is best remembered for the fact that in May 1932, he was dismissed from the office of Premier of New South Wales by the Governor-General.

At the beginning of 1941 only Britain, her Dominions and Colonies stood up against Hitler's war machine. France had succumbed all too easily and the United States was once more sitting uncommitted on the touchline. The action was in Europe and North

11

Africa. There was certainly the threat of war in South-East Asia but the bulk of the limited resources available to Britain and her allies was logically committed to stemming the tide in the west. Australia was drawn in too, not just because of historic or even family ties, but because of the reality that if the Suez Canal fell into the hands of Rommel's Afrika Corps, her isolation and vulnerability would have seemed complete. In August 1941 Robert Menzies's government fell, to be replaced by the Labor Party's John Curtin, a man who would prove to be anathema to both Roosevelt and Churchill. The attack on Pearl Harbor on 7 December 1941 and the Japanese threat posed from New Guinea, prompted Curtin to demand the recall of Australian naval assets and two of the three divisions in North Africa, in order to defend Australia. Shortly after the Australians had been withdrawn, Rommel rolled up the Allied forces in North Africa, culminating in the fall of Tobruk in June 1942.

Britain did defend the Malayan Peninsula and Singapore as well as the prevailing priorities would permit. The 840 men lost when the British battleship *Prince of Wales* and the venerable battle-cruiser *Repulse* were sunk off Kuantan, testify to an intention to defend Malaya. The loss of the heavy cruiser HMS *Exeter*, victor of the battle of the River Plate, in the Java Sea is evidence of an aspiration to defend Australia, albeit with resources so overstretched as to be ineffective. When Singapore fell to Japanese forces, Britain lost more than three times as many killed or captured as was suffered by Australia. It is true that Churchill had a broader strategic view than Labor Prime Minister John Curtin, but he did accede (with bad grace) to Curtin's insistent demand that the 7th Infantry Division, returning from the Western Desert, was not to be diverted to Burma. So, Curtin did get his troops back.

The Australia of 1942 was very different from the Australia of today. The vast influx of immigrants from all over the world, which has so changed the character and composition of Australian society in the years since the Second World War, had not even been foreseen let alone absorbed. The vast majority of the population came from British stock and the emotional links with Britain were still strong.

In the First World War, when many thousands of Australians gave their lives in France, Gallipoli and Palestine, the Australian showed himself to be a fighting man almost without peer, establishing a proud tradition which would live on when his country joined Britain in war in 1939 and throughout the six bitter years of triumphs and disasters which were to follow – at sea, on the land and in the air.

Briton and 'Digger' fought side by side against a common enemy. The rapid expansion of Australia's armed forces had left all too little for Home Defence and plans were perforce drawn up to abandon much of mainland Australia in the face of a Japanese advance which, providentially never occurred, although, as this book will tell, the Japanese did take the first tentative steps.

The chapters which follow provide an historic preamble which sets right Paul Keating's distorted view of Australia's military history as well as recording three occasions upon which Japanese forces clashed with Australia on the Australian mainland.

The research out on the ground in Australia was conducted through multiple visits to Broome, Cowra and Darwin during the two years 1984-86. For their help in putting the pieces together, I am grateful to the Broome Historical Society, Dr Duncan Anderson, Harry Gordon, Mervyn W Prime and Major W H Tyler, as well as to those mentioned by name in the text. The maps, and diagrams were drawn by André Effendi. Finally, for her help with the research, photography and preparation of the manuscript, I am, as usual, greatly indebted to Gina.

SEEDS

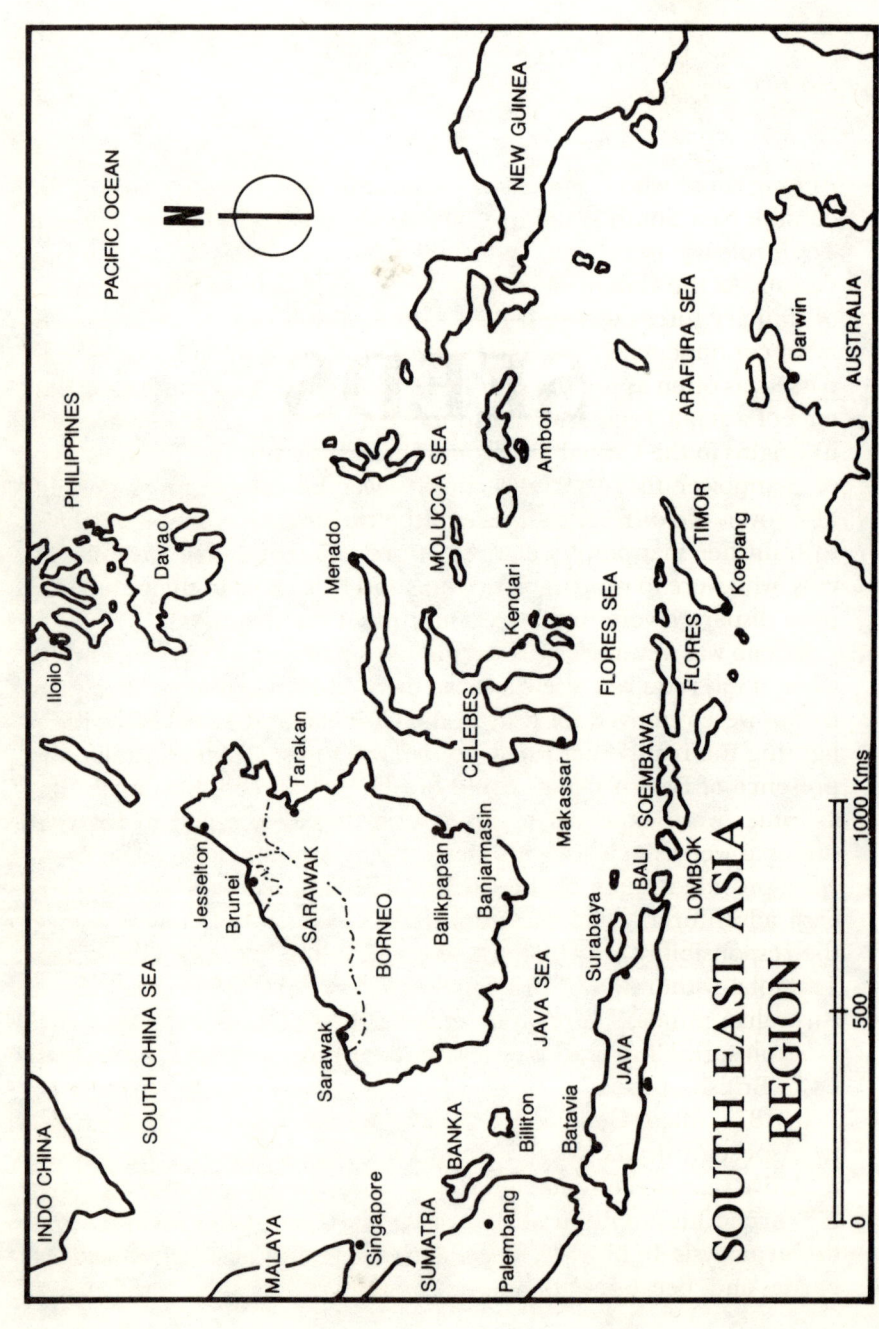

SOUTH EAST ASIA REGION

1. Seeds

Among those who disembarked when the First Fleet arrived off the coast of New South Wales in 1788 was a group of 200 Royal Marines. Their role was to protect the Colony from both internal and external threats. As the Colony developed, local responsibility for the finding of military forces was restricted to the raising of volunteer units to meet contingencies as and when they arose and, when the need had passed, as often as not the units were disbanded. This continuing pattern of a small, regular force, supported by volunteers, of course has its origins in the United Kingdom. The British, however, had reserves of manpower that Australia could never be capable of matching. Moreover, the difference in size of the two countries enabled Britain to train her manpower relatively more efficiently than the Australians, who were to remain hamstrung and frustrated in their efforts to train dispersed volunteers over infrequent training days.

Britain was never averse to taking her small garrison from Australia when it was required elsewhere. In the mid-19th century, the regular troops were removed for duty in the Crimean and Maori Wars, highlighting the reality that when no risk was foreseen for Australia, the presence of British troops could not be guaranteed. Eventually, the Colonies were expected to fund those forces assigned to internal duties as well as to assist with the cost of external defence. The Royal Navy provided much of the early umbrella to forestall external foreign adventurers. The exception was the control of coastal waters, the responsibility for which devolved upon the Colonies themselves. The total withdrawal of British ground forces in 1870 concentrated Australian minds. The land defence of the Colonies was passed to a random sprinkling of disparate volunteer units invariably commanded by British officers.

In 1877, Major-General Sir William Jervois arrived from England to inspect Australia's defences and to make a report. The Report took five years to compile, but it held good until Federation in 1901. He turned his attention to that perennial Australian chestnut – the threat analysis. In his view, the Colonies were only at risk from raiding parties and, because of the predomination of the Royal Navy, he saw no justification for anything other than small groups of regular forces, supported where necessary by a militia or volunteer reserve. In actual fact, few volunteer units were to survive, but some were merged into the militia, comprising partly-paid units whose organisation and training were carefully supervised. The militia therefore evolved as the dominant military force who, with the volunteers, comprised 95 per cent of the Colonial Forces at the time of Federation. These semi-professionals provided cost-effective forces to go to the Sudan in 1885, to the Boer War in 1899-1901, and to the Relief of Peking in 1900.

In 1889, another British officer, General Edwards, produced a revised threat-assessment, indicating that if war occurred in Europe, Australia would be attacked. He proposed that the varied and legally-impeded Colonial Forces should be federated so as to facilitate cross border co-operation and combined operations. In order to meet the new threat, Edwards proposed the establishment of a Federal force of 30-40,000 men. His Report was a political hot potato and did much to polarise attitudes that still prevail.

The 1890s were a period of great social and political tension. The frequent use of troops to break strikes engendered a hostility with the unions that lingers on. Union leaders saw, in the Federal Force argument, further licence for the bosses to use repressive measures against the work force. Throughout this phase of drought, depression and industrial strife, the social lobby was skilfully mobilised to encourage the Colonies to reduce their defence expenditure to the benefit of welfare. The traditional Anglophobia of the significant Irish Labor lobby emerged in its denunciations of the proposal to increase the size of the defence force as excuses to produce a reserve of Imperial cannon fodder. The objections were to become academic when the Colonial Defence Committee rejected Edwards' threat analysis, preferring to keep faith in the capabilities of the Royal Navy. The argument of benefits to be derived from a federated force therefore revolved less around operational efficiency as on the financial savings likely to accrue from centralising the defence forces.

Federation in 1901 introduced the Commonwealth Defence Forces as a component of the Commonwealth Ministry of Defence. Continuing economic depression, caused by drought, underlined the primacy of domestic issues over defence, with further cuts to the Commander-in-Chief's proposed forerunner of the Operational Defence Force. The shortage of funds brought the Army and Navy into conflict, with the Navy invariably emerging as winners. A 1911

report by the Royal Navy's Admiral Sir Reginald Henderson, underlined the clear threat posed by Japan and identified Australia's north
coast as their most likely landing point. The Army was left to soldier
on, to train as best it could with obsolete, indifferent and varied arms
and equipment. The Army's major success was organisational. The
disparate Colonial Forces were amalgamated into a force comprising
permanent and Citizen Military Forces (CMF). Military Districts were
created to command Garrison units utilising improving common
staff procedures.

The disasters of the Boer War had served to convince the significant band of Australian Defence opponents that the allocation of
monies to defence was a waste of limited financial resources which
could be better used in welfare areas. Fortunately, the shortcomings
highlighted during the Boer War had been noted, leading to the
Haldane Reforms in Britain. As was so often the case at this time,
what happened in the United Kingdom was to have implications for
Australia. As a result of the conclusions of the Imperial Conference,
1907, an Imperial General Staff was formed, with each Dominion
producing its own General Staff. Standard operating procedures and
documentation were evolved so that each Dominion force could slot
into others and operate as a concerted whole. The effect of this harmony was to reverse the earlier defence antithesis for, at heart, the
Australian people were loyal to the Crown and proud of their mem-
bership of the British Empire. There remained an extraordinary
'Britishness' about the population. The Australian writer and poet
Banjo Paterson related that half of those who made up the Australian
contingent of the Anzacs* at Gallipoli, a justifiably proud piece of
antipodean tradition, still retained the nationality of their country of
origin. In short, they were British.

Within 20 years of the rejection of Edwards' proposal for the establishment of a 30-40,000 strong force, the Kitchener Report proposed
and achieved universal military service to support a force of 80,000
men. Fortunate and opportune indeed had been the reforms, for
they enabled the Dominions to declare war as independent states, yet
march forward as a cohesive force into a conflict, the scale and ferocity of which would surpass the imagination.

In 1918, the soldiers of the Australian Imperial Forces (AIF) who
had been in the Great War, began slowly to trickle homeward on the
basis 'first out, first back'. The attitude at home was mixed. Bitterness

---

*ANZAC: Australian and New Zealand Army Corps.

and anger were universal, but these thoughts were tempered by pride that the skill and sacrifice of the Australian servicemen had shown the world that Australia had not only come of age but, more importantly, could stand on her own feet. The sacrifice had been tremendous. Of the number of soldiers engaged under British command, no country suffered higher casualties than Australia. 330,000 served overseas, of whom 226,073 became casualties – 68.5 per cent. That figure compared with New Zealand – 58 per cent, the United Kingdom – 52 per cent, and Canada – 51 per cent.

Throughout the cities, towns and farms of Australia there were many gaps at dining tables, places of sons who did not return from the War. The nation's youth had been whittled away, leaving much of the burden of earning the families' livelihood upon the shoulders of ageing parents. The impact upon Australia's industrial and rural development was severe but it could have been much worse. Two conscription referendums held in October 1916 and November 1917 were bitterly contested – the rejections were quite narrow – the Labor Party split along religious/ethnic lines (i.e. Irish Roman Catholics versus British Protestants). With the exception of the brief Scullin Government (1929-1931), the Labor Party was out of office from 1917 until Curtin's victory in 1941. The vote on conscription was extended to include the AIF in France. They voted against. They were very jealous of their unique, all volunteer status. Instead, Monash, one of the greatest Corps Commanders of the First World War, had to contend with fighting his volunteer Australian Corps starved of reinforcements. In the belief that the Great War had been 'the war to end all wars', Australians returned philosophically to the jobs that needed to be done.

Monash, the returning war hero, was invited by the Minister of Defence to head a committee to formulate future defence policy. In 1920, the Monash Report was delivered to the Minister. Secondary recommendations included the need to standardise railway gauges, the establishment of a military hierarchy, and the development of a logistic and materiel infrastructure. The main thrust of the report, however, was the identification of the threat and the measures required for that threat to be countered.

Monash and his committee had no doubt that there was but one future enemy – Japan. The suspicion of Japan was evident as early as 1897 but had grown into real fear by 1917-1920. Australia was violently opposed to Japan being granted League of Nations mandates over the German islands in the North Pacific – Truk is only 700 miles from Rabaul. Prime Minister Billy Hughes – much to the irritation of the Japanese – even argued against a clause enunciating racial equality in the League of Nations Charter. For the first time, serious questions were raised as to the wisdom of the dependence placed upon the Royal Navy. The thoughts were conjured of the relieving fleet having to steam 13,000 miles to be faced by a Japanese fleet already operating from the security of ports in Australia and Singapore. In 1904-1905, Russia had despatched an avenging fleet from the Baltic to the Sea of Japan. This epic voyage ended in catastrophic defeat at the hands of the Imperial Japanese Navy. The haunting spectre of another Tsushima was evident in the analysts' minds.

The committee assessed the strength of the Imperial Japanese Army to be 600,000 with a first lift capability of 100,000. Monash differed from Jervois in so far as he believed that the Japanese aim would be to invade and not simply to conduct raids. In examining the most likely objectives, the committee determined the Newcastle/Sydney/Melbourne areas to be vital and that their loss would be a mortal blow to Australia. It is significant that this early military analysis should exclude the city of Brisbane, and the territory to its north, from serious defence consideration.

In order to defend the populous south-east coast, the Report recommended a force of 270,000 supported by a peacetime army of 130,000. The influence of the citizen-soldier Monash was evident in the recommendation that the vast majority of the army would be CMF (Citizen Military Force), supplemented by only a small regular component. Universal conscription was seen as essential, with an eight-year training liability.

Military plans so often become superseded by events and more attractive political options. The Washington and Imperial Conferences of 1921 and 1923 sought to rationalise and reduce the world's armed forces. Australia was not slow in identifying herself with these desirable peace goals and set in motion the run-down of the Australian Defence Forces. The irony of this period, which also witnessed the decision to develop the Singapore Naval Base, was that it confirmed in Japan's mind the allied hostility against her. So, while the allies turned their attention to force reduction, Japan's planners were set upon force expansion. Meanwhile, in Australia, the Monash Report was filed away, the CMF was reduced to 40 per cent of its former strength, to 37,560 all ranks, while the regular army strength stood at a mere 1,600.

For the nation which had coined the *laissez-faire* phrases, 'she'll be right' and 'no worries', the inattention to military vigilance after the Great War, and failure to match a force structure to the threat, had come almost as second nature. Australia was, of course, not alone among those allies who relaxed their guard. The atmosphere of the age engendered a blind faith in the permanence of peace, and supreme optimism in the good offices of the League of Nations to resolve problems at the conference table. If those measures should fail, the remote island continent of Australia could naturally fall back on the untried linchpin of her defence, the Royal Navy.

The pendulum between morality and realism had swung heavily towards the former. The whole *raison d'être* of the League of Nations appealed to the moral ethos of the young sovereign state, who flexed her newly-acquired diplomatic muscle to align herself with the disarmament philosophy enshrined within the Covenant of the League.

During the period 1923-1930, the neglected CMF meandered forward, fuelled by a political logic which justified national security in terms of geographical isolation and the invincibility of the Royal Navy. There was a widely-held belief that it was a relatively simple matter to convert civilian to soldier, even though the AIF had required six months' training in 1915. No concessions were allowed for the emergent technology which would continue to complicate military science and justify an increase in the trianing bill. By the same token, the obvious shortage of soldiers on the ground in uniform was compensated for, in political minds, by the existence of a residual pool of trained manpower from the First World War. The fact that less than half of the returned soldiers were demobilised as fit, and that a significant number were now well into middle-age, seems to have escaped the body politic.

The meandering path was now in a downward spiral. The armed forces were starved of equipment, resources and incentive. In January 1930, the new Labor Government announced the disbandment of the CMF and its replacement by a militia with an annual training commitment of 16 days. This move coincided with an economic downturn which saw the planned defence expenditure for the next financial year fall below the relatively paltry sum of £4,000,000. Even the Royal Australian Navy (RAN) were not spared the economies, having to pay off five ships.

By 1933, the decline in defence fortunes stabilised when there was an infusion of defence monies. In 1938, the defence vote was doubled in order to match the looming threat of Germany – rather than Japan – which had become the focus of Australia's attention. The ceiling for the militia was raised to 70,000; a target which was achieved by March 1939. Again, Australia turned to Britain for her re-equipment and for a new Inspector-General. Some surprise was expressed that an Australian had not been selected for the appointment of Inspector-General, but Major-General Squires produced a sensible Report aimed at improving Australia's defence preparedness. A major proposal was for the formation of two regular brigades. The recommendation was accepted in principle by the Government, but the effect was to be diluted by committee and the money allocated instead to increasing the training of the militia.

Thus it was, at the prelude to war, that the Australian Army of 1939 was not dissimilar to that of 1914. It was inexperienced, desperately short of equipment, and that equipment which had been provided was largely obsolescent. Orders for new equipment had been belatedly placed on British industry, but this had coincided with Britain's own demands on an industrial base which had not been geared to rapid expansion.

*   *   *

It is my melancholy duty to inform you officially that, in consequence of a persistence by Germany in her invasion of Poland, Great Britain has declared war upon her and that, as a result, Australia is also at war.

When Robert Menzies informed the citizens of Australia that they were again at war it had been a bi-party decision, but the Australian Defence Force had suffered from the inability of successive governments to establish a balanced national force to match national needs. It was a 'defence' force in name only, for a significant component could not legally be deployed overseas.

The threads of Japan's involvement in the trilogy about to unfold had their origins in 1905. Russia's attempts to overwhelm this, the last of the unsubjugated Asian nations, went seriously awry. Her defeated and humiliated army was held at bay north of Mukden in Manchuria and her Second Pacific Squadron, as we have seen, had been destroyed at Tsushima, 'The Trafalgar of the East'. The Russo-Japanese war had bankrupted Japan both in financial and manpower terms, but she emerged confident and exceedingly ambitious. She sought in the American-sponsored peace talks at Portsmouth, New Hampshire, an honourable and generous settlement. Although she had won the war, she was to lose the peace, due in no small part to American public opinion siding with Christian Russia against heathen Japan. From this point can be identified the fatal rivalry which was to develop between the United States and Japan in the Pacific. The same Portsmouth peace conference, which was to so exasperate and frustrate Japan, was to confirm the United States as a major world force.

The armed forces of modern Japan had flourished and developed under the tutelage of the Royal Navy and Prussian Army. Britain and Japan had been allies throughout the Russo-Japanese War and their alliance was renewed in 1911, but herein lay an incongruity. It was a strange partnership for the world's premier colonial power to be associated with an Asian nation whose success in the conflict of arms against Russia should have initiated throughout the region the cry, 'Asia for the Asians'. It was Germany, however, who was first to feel the parting of the ways, in a most significant manner. Japan, who had never been involved in the origins of the Great War, declared war on Germany in 1914 and enterprisingly seized Germany's colonial interests in the Pacific and China. Britain took exception to these moves, believing that, as an ally of Japan, she should have been fully consulted.

British and American suspicions of Japanese regional aspirations were confirmed in 1915 when Japan presented China with the notorious 21 demands, virtually a plan for the annexation of China. The allies interceded to block the move, but there were some lonely voices asking whether it would not be wise to accommodate some of the Japanese ambitions within the region. In 1918, the assistant British Military Attaché in Peking wrote:

> If Japan is not given a free hand in some part of the Far East, there is a danger that she might actually go over to the enemy. With Russia a prostrate neutral between them, Japan and Germany would form an extremely strong combination, which could threaten the whole of the Allies' possessions in Asia and even in Australasia.

In 1918, a combined force, which included British, American and Japanese troops, had gone into Siberia to assist Admiral Kolchak's White Russians but, seeing the pointlessness of the exercise, Britain and the United States withdrew; Japan remained until 1922.

Japan regarded the series of conferences in the early 1920s, aimed at force reduction and arms control, as being designed to prevent her rightful expansion. The first Washington Conference in 1921 established a ratio of warship tonnages between Britain, the United States and Japan in the ratio 5:5:3. In 1923 Britain, encouraged by the United States, abrogated her alliance with Japan thereby ending, among other things, technical exchange. Japan's hawkish posture was to prevail, as further limitations on the Imperial Japanese Navy were applied during the two Naval Conferences of 1930 and 1935. Japan's disdain and low regard of the Anglo-Saxon alliance was fostered by Britain's decision in 1924 to develop the Singapore Naval Base, and the United States' ban during the same year on further Japanese immigration. All this appeared to a xenophobic Japan to smack of collusion to prevent Japan from assuming her rightful place in world affairs. In February 1933, the League of Nations censured Japan's involvement in the 1931 Manchurian Incident. As a result, the Japanese delegation withdrew from the League.

In January 1936, Japan dissociated herself from the restrictions imposed on fleet sizes. She then embarked upon a massive shipbuilding programme to the extent that by 1941 she had achieved parity with the United States' Navy. Furthermore, because her navy was operating in the one region, she could deploy in the Pacific a larger, more modern fleet than the combined assets of Great Britain, the United States, Australia and the Netherlands.

The Japanese invasion of China in 1937 was the actual beginning of the War in the Far East* or, what Japan preferred to describe as the 'Greater East Asian Co-Prosperity Sphere'. Britain and America protested at the violation of Chinese sovereignty but, short of declaring war, they remained powerless to intervene. Japan's invasion of China developed into a beneficial exercise area for Japanese forces and their equipment in much the same way that Spain was used as Germany's proving ground. For Japan, the need for quality technical assistance took on a new urgency and there was only one country who could satisfy her needs – Germany. After the outbreak of war in Europe in 1939, Japan developed closer ties with Germany, culminating in the signing of the Tripartite Pact in September 1940.

Vichy France acquiesced in Japan's request to occupy Indo-China to act as a further lever upon China, but this move was to have serious repercussions. As a counter measure, Britain, the United States and the Netherlands froze Japanese assets, which effectively halted the flow of oil into the country. No other single act could have been more certain to escalate an already volatile situation. Japan's oil paranoia had developed as early as the 1920s. Shipping, which included a much expanded Imperial Navy and a merchant fleet which, between 1918-1924, had grown by 80 per cent, had changed from being coal-

---

* In *An Intellectual History of Wartime Japan 1931-1945* (pp37-38), Shunsuke Tsurumi suggests that 'The Fifteen Year' War began in 1931.

to oil-fired. It was these ships which became crucial in sustaining an export-dependent economy. Activities to seek out alternative fuel supplies reached frenetic proportions during 1926-1927. Japan's whole future relied upon continual access to substantial oil reserves. Without oil, Japan could not continue the war against China, so she considered her options.

The oilfields of the Dutch East Indies were a rich prize. To seize them would involve a substantial escalation of the war effort as well as taking prodigious maritime risks. Some in the Japanese hierarchy regarded conflict with the Western Alliance as inevitable. It was also argued that an attack on the Dutch East Indies would be in accordance with medium-term plans to develop a co-prosperity sphere. There was no denying that without a guaranteed supply of oil, the lengthy war in China could not be brought to a satisfactory conclusion. Thus, a simple though effective retaliatory act determined the course of the war in the Pacific; a war which would bring Japanese ground forces within a few hundred kilometres of Australia's northern coastline.

In 1939, history repeated itself. As in 1914, when Britain went to war, so did the Dominions. It all seemed quite natural. On 15 September 1939, Robert Menzies announced the commencement of recruiting for the Second AIF, an all-volunteer force which would serve either at home or abroad 'as circumstances permit'. By 1941, the AIF had grown to four divisions. The Sixth, Seventh and Ninth Divisions, comprising the First Australian Corps, were serving with great distinction in North Africa and the eastern Mediterranean, while the newly-raised Eighth Division was deploying to Malaya. Of these four Australian divisions, Churchill wrote that they:

> were composed of the flower of their military manhood across the world to aid the Mother Country in the war, in the making of which and in the want of preparations for which they had to share.

At sea, the Royal Australian Navy gave a lead to her elder sister, the Royal Navy. On 19 June 1940, only nine days after Italy's declaration of war, the light cruiser HMAS *Sydney* located, chased and sank the Italian heavy cruiser *Bartolomeo Colleoni* in emulation of the first *Sydney's* sinking of the German cruiser *Emden* 24 years earlier. No less distinguished was the performance of many Royal Australian Air Force pilots, whom the Luftwaffe soon found to be tough and resilient adversaries. Critics in Australia were to condemn the deployment to the eastern Mediterranean as being in Britain's, rather than

Australia's interests. The fact remains that the experience arising from this deployment gave Australia well-trained, battle-hardened forces who, when redeployed to the Pacific, were to stop the Japanese advance at Milne Bay and on the Kokoda Track.

By later 1941, the reserves of trained AIF manpower in Australia had been well nigh exhausted – the war was entering its third year and the flow of volunteers was beginning to diminish. Australia did have a large conscript Militia, but these troops could not be sent outside Australian territory. The RAN was hard-pressed to dominate the sea lines of communications, there were very few troops remaining who could legally be deployed abroad, and the RAAF had to contend with old and unreliable aircraft. This parlous situation was all very well as long as the war remained at arm's length in distant Europe.

On 19 November 1941, HMAS *Sydney* was lost with all hands off the west coast of Australia. She had closed to investigate what proved to be the *Kormoran*, a German 'Q' ship. There is still some suggestion that the 'Q' ship was working covertly in tandem with a Japanese submarine. While plausible, it appears unlikely that such a secret would have endured the passage of time. HMAS *Sydney* suffered fatal damage and had problems with her damage control. After she had broken off the engagement, she was never seen again. All that was ever found was one Carley float, which is now in the Australian War Memorial, Canberra. The loss of the *Sydney* in Australian waters sounded an ominous warning to those who believed that a cosy security buffer existed in their distance from what was then the seat of a European war.

The Australian homeland was protected by the Militia, a force of 200,000 men which in October 1939 had been expanded by the introduction of compulsory military service. A political sleight of hand had extended the homeland to include New Guinea in order to overcome the traditional resistance to conscripts serving overseas. A Militia was, therefore, free to be deployed to Papua.

When Japan occupied Indo-China, a decision was taken to deploy the Australian Eighth Division to Singapore, an area considered by Australia to be within her own defensive sphere of interest. Singapore became the key element in a forward Australian strategy. The 'Lion City' is, after all, the same distance from Darwin as is Melbourne. In December 1941, Curtin warned Churchill that any thoughts of evacuating Singapore would be regarded as 'an inexcusable betrayal'. Also during 1941 and early 1942, troops were deployed to Rabaul, Ambon and Timor, while a Militia battalion was sent to

Port Moresby (in New Guinea) as a preliminary to establishing a Militia brigade there. Australia's growing concern for the developments in her own region was reflected in her refusal to provide reinforcements to General Blamey in the Middle East. The priority now was not to enhance existing operational commitments but to concentrate on the defence of the Australian homeland.

During the first week of December 1941, a proliferation of intelligence indicators pointed towards the inevitability of the attack on Pearl Harbor. At about 7am on the morning of 7 December, the radar station at Oahu intercepted the signals of a force of an estimated one hundred aircraft approaching from the north. This movement was interpreted by an inexperienced officer as being twelve B-17s which were expected to arrive from the east.

When the Japanese carrier *Akagi* triggered the attack against the Americans, she flew from her masthead the same faded battle flag which had once flown aboard Togo's flagship *Mikasa* when he led the pre-emptive attacks against the Russians at Port Arthur in 1904. On that occasion too, the Japanese had side-stepped the niceties of a declaration of war, showing that they had also learned from their British naval instructors in general, and Nelson in particular, the benefits of having a navy sufficiently strong to attack the enemy in their own port. Unlike the British and Britain's allies, however, Japan had perceived the superiority of airpower over battleships and battle cruisers.

Allied operational analysis of the effects of bombing had been based largely on studies of strategic bombing in the European theatre. It had been observed that in night raids against Germany in 1941, less than ten per cent of bombs fell within five miles of the target. The success of the Luftwaffe against, perhaps, the more relevant Royal Navy targets off the Norwegian and Dunkirk coasts was largely overlooked. Indeed, it was to be the blindness to these significant developments in air warfare of the newly-arrived Commander-in-Chief Far East, Admiral Sir Tom Phillips, which was to prove fatal. Phillips persistently maintained that properly-trained naval gun crews could repel any form of air attack.

The Japanese, however, had been shrewd observers of the emerging military scene. They developed their own naval attack concepts from a seed sown by, of all people, the Royal Navy, as a result of the successful torpedo attack on the Italian Navy at Taranto in 1940. The Japanese integrated their carrier-borne airforce with land-based air forces, operating as a concerted whole. Carrier and land-based pilots were keen and eager, having derived considerable benefit and experience from the four years of war against China. They became masters of pinpoint bombing. A potent addition to their armoury was a secret, revolutionary, oxygen-propelled torpedo. It had at least four times the range of the best British and American torpedoes, had a heavier warhead, was faster and left no tell-tale wake.

The attack on the United States' Navy at Pearl Harbor on Sunday, 7 December 1941, was to have a profound effect on future events at sea, in the air and on the land within the Australasian-South East Asian region. Concurrent attacks were launched against Malaya and Hong Kong, although the International Date Line distorts this concurrency to show it occurring on Monday, 8 December. To demonstrate the growth of Australian nationalism, Curtin's government did not wait for Britain to declare war on Japan before doing so.

The neutralising of the American fleet, 'a day of infamy', had been essential in order to give Japan any prospect of success in her progress towards her ultimate objective of Java. The quality of the Japanese war machine was gravely underestimated by the Allies. Had the two countries not been at peace, and had the American fleet been prepared – and not caught by surprise in a congested harbor – then the outcome would have been entirely different. 'Made in Japan' conjured an impression of a shoddy copy of the Western product. While it was known that the Japanese did possess in the Zero what appeared to be an impressive little fighter, and while equally and undeniably she had a very modern navy, it was assumed that the Japanese would not have the ability to employ this modern equipment to best effect. As so often before in the history of warfare, the price to be paid by the Americans for grossly under-estimating their enemy was devastating.

Singapore Naval Base was a base in name only. When first established in 1921, the spread of Axis power could not have been imagined. The fifteen-inch fortress guns impotently overlooked a sea approach which would not be used, while Yamashita's Twenty-Fifth Army approached Singapore's back door by two axes of advance down the Malayan Peninsula.

At the outbreak of war with Japan, the Royal Navy had what would prove to be but a token force in the Far East. The terrible attrition inflicted upon the Royal Navy in the first years of the war could not have been foreseen. The vortex of the Atlantic and Mediterranean sucked in Royal Navy ships from the Indian and Pacific Oceans, never to return again as a significant force. The Americans remained coy as to the value of the Singapore base, sharing Wavell's view that it was indefensible. Such was the state of regional, naval co-operation and joint national planning that the American Asiatic fleet was not permitted to operate under Royal Navy orders.

In response to the Japanese landings in Siam and Malaya, Admiral Phillips manoeuvred his fleet in the area of the Gulf of Siam. On 10 December, the modern battleship HMS *Prince of Wales*, accompanied by the 25 year old battlecruiser HMS *Repulse* and an escort of four destroyers, were off the Malay town of Kuantan. *Repulse* had been speedily recalled from a 'flag showing' courtesy visit proposed for Darwin. Britain was at war with Japan. Churchill's 'decisive deterrent force', also known as 'Z' Force, was alert, prepared for action and in fighting trim, with sea room to manoeuvre. The major problem was the fleet's lack of air cover. The group's carrier, HMS *Indomitable*, had gone aground on 3 November 1941 at the entrance to Kingston Harbour, Jamaica, but Phillips placed supreme reliance upon what was thought to be a comprehensive on-board, anti-aircraft defence system, as well as the residue of RAF aircraft operating from the airfields of north Malaya.

Such had been the impact of the surprise Japanese landings that the remaining out-gunned and out-manoeuvred RAF planes were being withdrawn southward. The way had therefore been left open for 84 Japanese torpedo planes and bombers to tear the two capital ships apart. Seven torpedoes struck the *Prince of Wales*, and twice that number sank the *Repulse*. Only three Japanese planes were lost in this naval disaster, which is said to have had a greater impact on Churchill's morale than any other single disaster of the war. It had been a day that had confirmed the demise of the big-gunned ships. It was a day that signalled the potency of the Japanese armed forces. Not one Allied capital ship now remained in the region to obstruct Japanese designs on the Dutch East Indies. Finally, it had dispelled the illusion of an Australian strategy which had been based upon the pre-eminence and protection of the Royal Navy. For the first time in centuries, the Royal Navy had lost its superiority in a theatre of war at sea and the United States was there, willing to fill the vacuum.

John Curtin became Prime Minister of a Labor Government on 7 October 1941. Within months, indeed weeks, the perspective of war in the region would take on a new focus in both its immediacy and its proximity. Australians looked to the north in horror as countries on the periphery of their own immediate area of defence interest were being systematically devoured by the Japanese juggernaut.

The American Consul in Adelaide reported the sense of panic that arose when the news of the loss of the Royal Navy ships spread through the city:

> Staid businessmen who only the day before were complacent about the menace of the 'yellow dwarf' were now reduced almost to wringing their hands.

The American Ambassador in Canberra conveyed his impression to Roosevelt:

> One gets the feeling that Australia was ready to give up without a struggle; that if it had been possible to leave the country the people would have gone.

Posters appeared with 'He's coming south', emblazoned upon them. The need to explain who 'he' was happened to be superfluous since Australia possessed an ingrained fear of Asiatic aggression.

Hong Kong fell on 26 December 1941 and, on 23 January 1942, the loss of Rabaul brought the enemy to the very doorstep of Australia. Allied efforts to cobble together their disparate forces into an harmonious whole had so far been frustrated. First, by local commanders lacking the authority to make the necessary decisions and secondly, through national concern either to retain or maximise their own national authority. It was therefore something of a surprise that Roosevelt should uncharacteristically nominate the former British Commander-in-Chief India, General Sir Archibald Wavell, to command the naval, land and air assets of America, Britain, the Netherlands and Australia in South-East Asia. The British Cabinet agreed to the American proposal and on 15 January the new command, ABDA, was established, drawing its name from the national constituents: American, British, Dutch and Australian forces. The failure to involve the Australians and Dutch in the discussions held in Washington between Churchill and Roosevelt caused simmering resentment. The British also maintained the suspicion that they had been duped into allowing one of their generals to lead what was likely to be a lost cause.

Of the naval strength available, HMS *Exeter*, one of the victors of the Battle of the River Plate, and USS *Houston*, were the only two heavy cruisers in the region. *Exeter* was a casualty of the Washington Naval Limitation Treaty. Resultant obligatory design changes left her shorter, and therefore less well protected, than was originally planned. Also within this varied and unco-ordinated force were a further 11 light cruisers and a mixed bag of destroyers and submarines. The enforced move of the Command from Singapore to Dutch Java merely served to highlight smouldering Netherlands' resentment of the appointment of an American Admiral, Thomas Hart, to command the combined naval forces. He was a highly professional man who had joined his new command aboard the submarine USS *Shark* with other refugees from Manila. His optimism was to be dulled by infighting, a remote headquarters, and poor communications. Had there been better co-ordination, harmony, and an integrated command structure, the Allied disaster at sea which was about to unfold might have been avoided.

Wavell did his utmost to deploy the limited land forces available to him to the best effect. This was not always achieved. The last-minute despatch of troops to Singapore, for example, only served to add to the confusion and to the size of the loss. Wavell's deputy, the American General Brett, endeavoured to persuade Australia to deploy additional troops to Timor; a proposal which was to be met by stern resistance. Churchill and Curtin had agreed, concurrently, to redeploy the Second AIF from the Middle-East to the South-East Asian theatre, but the deteriorating events in Singapore forced a reappraisal, yet one which produced widely divergent solutions.

For the Allies, the fall of Singapore on 15 February was a catastrophic event of massive proportions. Even in 1905, when Japan had defeated and humiliated Russia, the Russian Army had been spared the ignominy of surrender. The British surrender and the loss of that jewel of the Empire, the Lion City, to an Asiatic race, marked the end of an era. This had not been simply the loss of a battle, but a humiliating defeat of the leading colonial power. It was a reversal from which Britain would not recover. The total Japanese casualties for the entire Malay-Singapore campaign had been 9,824 against an Allied loss, killed or taken into captivity, of 138,708. 17,000 men were of the Australian Eighth Division but over five times that number of Britons lost their lives or suffered the hell of captivity. 45,000 of the 50,000* Indians who surrendered in Malaya and Singapore joined the Japanese-sponsored Indian National Army. The Gurkhas remained loyal to the British. This does much to explain the 'crisis of confidence' which beset British imperialism from February 1942 onwards. Japan, surprised by the speed and size of her victory, absorbed the mineral resources of the region and developed the newly-won strategic assets in preparation for the next phase of dispossessing the Dutch colonial power of their jewel – the island of Java.

---

* Stanley L. Falk, *Seventy Days to Singapore: Malayan Campaign 1941-1942*, (London 1975), pp263-264.

Stunned by the rapidity of the Japanese advance, Curtin made urgent contact with Churchill on 15 and 17 February. He proposed that the Australian troops be withdrawn from the Middle-East and deployed to their homeland. The situation in Burma was also grave and Wavell had hoped to use some of the returning Australians to stem the tide of the Japanese advance in that country. The Americans, themselves in the process of being evicted from the Philippines, had agreed to put a division into Australia as a *quid pro quo* for the Australian reinforcement of Burma. Events which would unfold at Darwin were to strengthen Curtin's resolve to oppose the diversion of Australian troops to Burma. Churchill's arbitrary re-routing of the Australian Twenty-First Brigade to Rangoon fuelled the developing political rift between Canberra and London. It was a confrontation from which Churchill backed off, confirming Australia's growing independence and divorce from Britain.

This was to be a period of rapid re-polarisation. General Douglas MacArthur's arrival on 17 March at Batchelor, south of Darwin, following his much-publicised escape from the Philippines, was a significant omen, seemingly underlining the actual shift of Allied power that had occurred in the region. For Australia, it was a new beginning, a new and lasting defence realignment that had grown out of the vacuum left by a defeated Britain and the circumstantial filling of that void, almost accidentally, by the United States. The seal had been set on Australia's growing disillusionment with a Britain which had persistently derided Australia's fears of a Japanese threat. Prime Minister Curtin had announced in his New Year message in December 1941, that Australia looked 'to America, free of any pangs as to her traditional links or kinship with the United Kingdom'.

The Japanese invasion plan for the Dutch East Indies was based on a three-pronged assault converging upon the island of Java. The Western force, operating out of Indo-China, had the intermediate objective of Palembang in Southern Sumatra, with Western Java the ultimate goal. A central force, operating from Davao in the Philippines, was to seize the South Borneo oilfields en route to Java. Davao was also to be the launch-pad for an eastern force, with the aim of mopping up Celebes, Ambon and Timor.

Timor had no immediate significance in the central Japanese plan of seizing Java. The importance of this small island was its strategic position in relation to the sea route from Java to Australia. However, the port of Darwin, on Australia's northern coastline, was a crucial consideration. They had investigated the feasibility of a land assault against the continent of Australia. The Imperial Japanese Navy spoke in favour of the occupation of Australia to deny its use for American-led counter measures against Japan. The Japanese Army, already suffering the effects of overstretch, argued that they would need ten divisions to secure Australia, ten divisions which they did not have. Darwin, however, had grown to be a large American and Australian logistic base supporting the Dutch East Indies. The port provided the only significant harbour along the entire, long, empty, northern coastline, and her airfields enabled Allied aircraft to sally forth into the Java Sea.

DARWIN

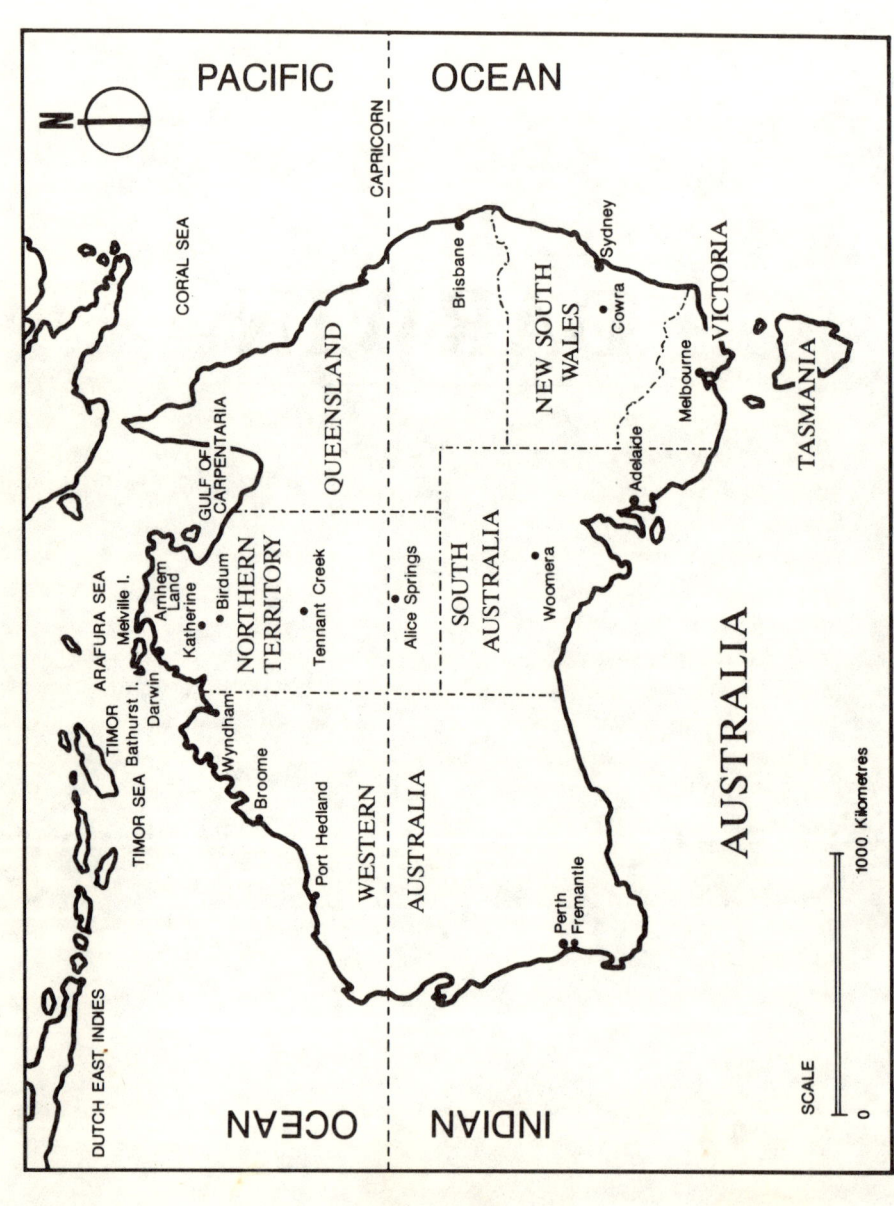

2. Darwin

The Northern Territory of Australia, of which Darwin is the capital, is 1,346,200 square kilometres of open space. It comprises approximately one sixth of the Australian continent, yet is inhabited by less than three-quarters of one per cent of the Australian population. Most of the Territory lies within the torrid zone of the Tropic of Capricorn. With but one exception, there is no one area naturally suited to intensive settlement. Much of the land is semi-arid with a massive expanse of sand dune and claypan desert, forming part of Australia's 'dead heart'. The exception is a strip of the coastal belt which is, in places, lush and green with semi-tropical vegetation.

The two seasons, 'the wet' and 'the dry', regulate life in the Territory. The hot summer period from October to April is the rainy season, but most of the average rainfall (up to 127 centimetres a year) comes during the four months from December to March. This is a period of high humidity and overcast skies, when it is not unusual for it to rain every day, the torrential rain being frequently brought in by the north-west monsoon winds. The rivers and streams flood, disrupting communications or making them very difficult. The 'wet' is synonymous with the 'cyclone season', and Darwin falls within the southern zone of tropical revolving storms. On Christmas Day 1974, *Cyclone Tracy* destroyed 90 per cent of Darwin's houses in one of the worst natural disasters ever to befall Australia.

The dry season from May to September is more benevolent and features warm, cloudless days ending in brilliant moonlit tropical nights. It rarely rains during the dry season, hence communications and supply are seldom a problem. The maximum temperature in the coastal region is approximately 30 degrees Centigrade, rising to 40 degrees in the 'wet'.

European contact with the Northern Territory can be traced to 1623 through the log of the Dutch ship *Arnhem*, from which Arnhem Land was named. British interest in the region was aroused by the fear of French settlement and the increase in Dutch trade. Initial efforts in the early 19th century to establish settlements on the inhospitable north coast were frustrated by the harsh climate, poor soil, and the very real problem of isolation. The formal possession of the land of the Northern Territory was taken in the name of King George IV by Captain Gordon Bremer on 20 September 1824.

'Port Darwin' was so named by Lieutenant J L Stokes RN on 9 September 1839. He anchored his ship HMS *Beagle,* in what is now known as Shoal Bay, and set off in a longboat with a Lieutenant Forsyth to explore the vast 1,000 square kilometre natural harbour. Given a tide range of almost 8 metres, the significance of this ready-made harbour was not lost on the two officers. They negotiated mangrove swamps infested by estuarine crocodiles and plagues of mosquitoes until they came to the base of a cliff, which they climbed. They surveyed the vast extent of the harbour in the early morning sunshine, and so impressed was Stokes that he decided to name the harbour 'Port Darwin' after his friend, the biologist Charles Darwin. It had, wrote Stokes, 'afforded us an opportunity of convincing an old shipmate that he still lived on in our memory'.

Exploration and development was a slow business, but much of the pioneering was overland, coming from the south. Over a period of time, responsibility for the Territory was to pass from the mother colony of New South Wales to South Australia, and thence to Commonwealth Government control through the offices of an appointed Administrator. The Territory was finally granted self-government on 1 July 1978. From this point, it is now necessary to retrace our steps, to return to Darwin in early 1942.

* * *

By February 1942, the inhabitants of the frontier town of Darwin had not come through the 'wet's' enervating heat, humidity and frustrations as well as they normally would have expected. The town exuded an air of impatience and tension. Communications were never good and this served only to exacerbate the situation. As the land route to the south was invariably closed by the elements at this time of the year, dependence for supply rested upon the arrival of a steamer every two months. The looming Japanese threat to the Dutch islands to the north raised a big question-mark as to how long this artery would remain open.

The narrow-gauge North Australia railway ran 544 kilometres south of Darwin to Birdum, yet from here to the next nearest railway station at Alice Springs was a further 800 kilometres. It was originally intended that the railway running south from Darwin should terminate 76 kilometres to the south of Birdum at Daly Waters but further progress was stopped by the economic depression. The resultant gap was covered by an indifferent and unsealed road, invariably impassable in 'the wet'. The road from Darwin to Adelaide River, a distance of 117 kilometres was, however, kept in a reasonable state of repair. The civil airfield at Parap was very much the poor relation to the larger RAAF airbase which lay some four kilometres away. The air routes had been barely developed, planes being both small and infrequent. After the members of a Royal Commission had been hurriedly convened to investigate the alleged occurrences about to unfold in Darwin, their flight from Melbourne took two days. Little wonder that those in Darwin felt their isolation so acutely.

Shortages of food and petrol were already making an impact. This had caused a growing resentment of the military by the civilians. Petrol supply was so bad that the locals were unable to go about their normal business. Customers were obliged to queue for hours at the pumps on a 'first come, first served' basis, and even then they were restricted to two gallons. Restaurants and cafés were short of food but, much worse, bars ran short of beer. In order to preserve stocks of food and drink for the civilian population, eating and drinking houses were placed out of bounds to the troops. The protest was immediate and emphatic. Servicemen went on a rampage verging on a riot as they vented their anger on the town's inhospitality.

It is a significant occurrence in the initial phase of a war that the military bureaucrat is often replaced by the warrior. This reflects the different attributes and qualities required by a general in war as opposed to peace. Leadership is no less important in Government. Some peace-time administrators, as do some peace-time generals, make the transition from peace to war with consummate ease. The very isolation and remoteness of Darwin and the Northern Territory would place added emphasis on the need for exemplary leadership in the event that war should occur. The need was for a respected, vigorous, alert achiever to tease out of the local bureaucrats suitable contingency plans for what a significant proportion of the population now regarded as the inevitability of war. The Civil Administrator was in effect the governor of the Northern Territories, although he had no powers over the military. He ought to have been a charismatic man, exercising an harmonious influence upon the disparate and, in many cases, limited leaders of the diverse civilian factions and Service groups. Above all, he would require energy, sympathy, commitment and interest to lead the population.

Instead, Darwin had in its resident Administrator, Charles Lydiard

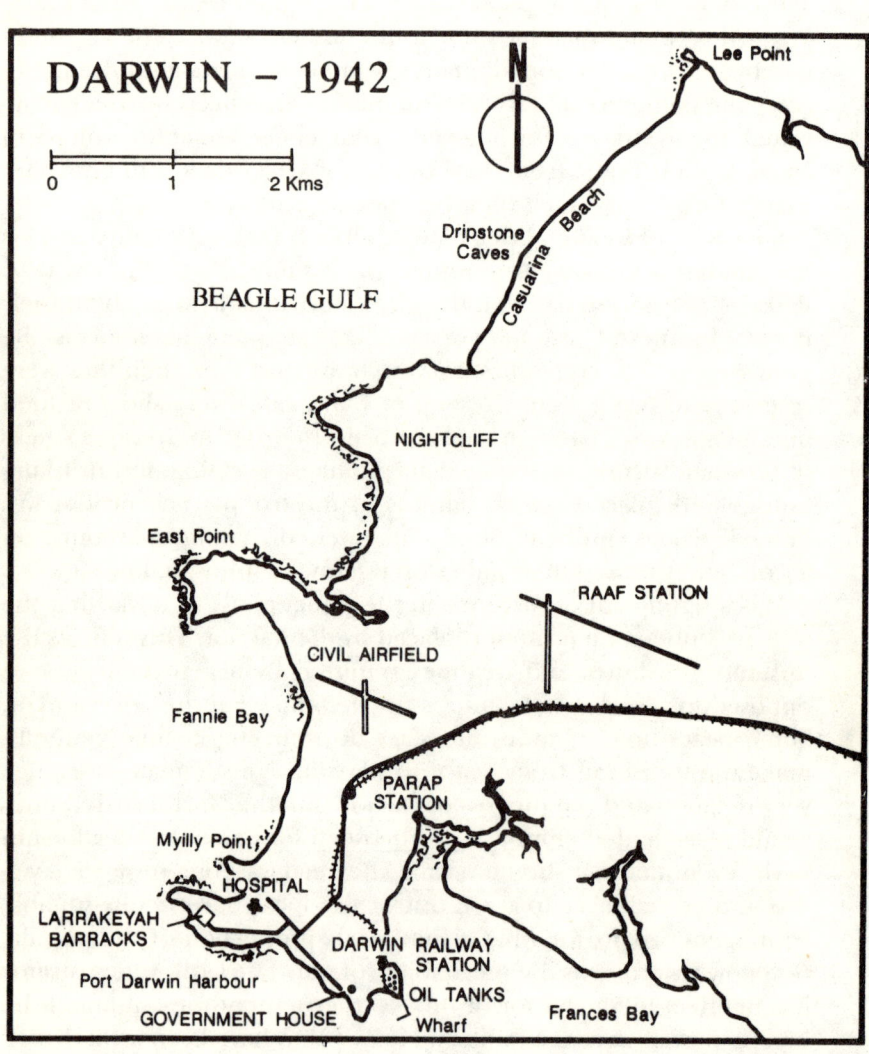

DARWIN – 1942

0   1   2 Kms

N

Lee Point

BEAGLE GULF

Dripstone
Caves

Casuarina Beach

NIGHTCLIFF

East Point

RAAF STATION

CIVIL AIRFIELD

Fannie Bay

PARAP
STATION

Myilly Point

HOSPITAL

LARRAKEYAH
BARRACKS

DARWIN RAILWAY
STATION

Port Darwin Harbour

OIL TANKS

GOVERNMENT HOUSE

Wharf

Frances Bay

Aubrey Abbott, an aloof, socially aware, remote and uncommunicative man. He had been a Country Party Minister for Home Affairs in the 1928-1929 Bruce-Page government. He resigned his seat of Gwydir to assume the appointment as Territory Administrator in 1937. Now aged 55, he lived with his wife Hilda in the seven-gabled Government House. The house, built in 1869, still stands, impressive yet isolated on a promontory luxuriating in arboreal shade. The Administration offices adjoined the house, which meant that Abbott could, if he wished, isolate himself from a community with which he so much differed and, in the main, deprecated. The relations between the Northern Australian Workers' Union and Abbott were intensely frigid. The greatest object of Abbott's disdain, the very antithesis of what he represented, lay at the foot of the cliffs below his house. This was the docks and wharf area. The operatives, 'wharfies', were a rough, belligerent bunch of highly-politicised men, whose restrictive practices frustrated business and military men alike. They were never slow to stop work or strike, which brought their loyalty into question at a time when their country was at war.

To some degree they were a maligned group who could have responded to better leadership. Their work was hot, difficult, unpopular and poorly-paid. Additional labour had had to be recruited from Perth in order to increase the number of gangs to work the burgeoning number of ships using the harbour and docks facilities.

The jetty was 'L' shaped, with the main arm of the quay in the deep water, running parallel to the shore. Along the length of the jetty ran the water and fuel pipes. This meant that the unloading of ships, difficult in itself due to the substantial rise and fall of the tide, would be interrupted when other ships arrived to be victualled. A railway followed the length of the pier but, at the right-angle, there was a turntable at which railway trucks had to be manhandled through 90 degrees before being released into congested sidings along the shore. This was hardly the most efficient dock for Australia's frontline port. That same conclusion had been reached by a visiting inspector two months previously, but the implementation of his recommendations would come too late to ease the problem of congestion in the harbour and the resultant destruction.

Abbott had served in the Great War and so should have been attuned to the need for preparation in the transition to war. Instead, he allowed himself to become isolated, besotted by his own newfound status. He was attended upon by a large staff, both in his superb house and in the adjoining offices. In a shed at the railway station was his personal 36-ton carriage, to be used when he toured the Territory within the confines of an extremely limited railway system.

The Administrator's first test of strength with the militant North Australia Workers' Union had resulted in a humiliating defeat. In 1918 the Union had seen off one of Abbott's predecessors, Dr JA Gilruth. Abbott attempted to use a group of public servants to break a strike on the wharf by unloading a strike-bound ship. Earlier attempts to use servicemen to unload strike-bound ships had proved counter productive. His heavy-handed tactic failed. Three days later, the ship sailed, still loaded, leaving a victorious yet embittered union. Abbott fared no better with those with whom it might be thought he enjoyed a closer association. His immediate subordinates in the public service found him difficult to work for. Some resigned and some persevered unhappily.

It should be remembered that Abbott had no political affinity with the socialist Curtin government. He was therefore not restrained by political niceties from making the strongest representations to provide for the glaringly obvious needs of a town about to be embroiled in war. Of the Administrator, the local judge TA Wells said: 'People find it very difficult to deal with Abbott because he is a man whose word you cannot depend upon, and they are right'. Well's disdain for the Administrator was reciprocated by Abbott who found that the judge's incaution, ambiguities and prejudices added nothing to the Territory's judicial reputation. However, Abbott's difficulty cannot be better demonstrated than in the important area of Civil Defence.

In June 1940, a group of concerned citizens approached Abbott to establish a Civil Defence organisation. The Administrator agreed to the proposals and accordingly the town was divided into zones, and zone wardens appointed. The attitude of many residents to the wardens was both cynical and unco-operative. They became irked by the wardens' weekly checks to ensure that the nominal rolls of residents reflected arrivals and departures. The compilation of the registers had been done competently and diligently, going so far as to categorise the 6,000 population according to sex, age and health. In time, the townspeople became irritated by the Civil Defence organisation, whose members they identified as troublesome, inquisitive, do-gooding busybodies, intruding unnecessarily into their leisure and privacy.

On 12 December, the day after the first false air-raid alarm and five days into the Pacific War, a deputation of Civil Defence officers called on Abbott. The visitors requested the immediate grant of statutory powers to give them the necessary authority to carry out their work. Abbott did nothing, for he feared that such a measure might lead to panic. As a compromise, however, he acceded to their second request by asking the Prime Minister for the authority to evacuate the elderly, infirm, women and children. This request was endorsed on the same day by the War Cabinet, who ruled that it would be carried out at public expense – yet legal authority to enforce the evacuation was never given.

While efforts were well under way to move the docile rump of non-essential citizens, the Civil Defence body persevered in their attempt to achieve legal standing. The necessary authority could have been provided by a local Ordinance should the Administrator have been of a mind to recommend the measure to the Governor-General. However, of that mind he was not and, following three weeks of procrastination, a public meeting resolved to send a telegram to both the Prime Minister and Minister for the Interior demanding Abbott's removal from office. The signals had little effect on the Government for the telegrams were not unique in the history of the robust relations between Administrators and the irreconcilable factions in the wild north. The Minister for the Interior, Abbott's immediate superior, even went on record to dismiss the citizen's demands by describing them as a fit of pique brought about by a shortage of beer.

The bulk of the population needed no prompting to evacuate. Ships that took away the greater proportion of the townspeople included the *President Grant,* whose arrival from war-torn Manila proved to be fortuitous. Of the 2,000 civilians who still remained immediately prior to the attack on Darwin, only 63 were women, performing so-called 'essential duties'. Among that number were nurses and post office employees.

The Civil Defence officers found to their dismay that a significant proportion of those who chose to remain were the intransigent disbelievers. They could not be persuaded that a threat existed, of the need to dig slit trenches or to comply with black-out regulations. Inevitably, the situation led to violence.

Abbott was now also under pressure from the Citizens' War Effort Committee, which had accused him of negligence in the provision of supplies. Demands to authorise the provision of sandbagged first-aid posts met with similar apathy. To add to the pressure, an ultimatum from all wardens was lodged at the Administrator's Office insisting that if, within three days, they had not been given statutory and legal rights to conduct their voluntary activities, they would resign. Abbott did not deign to reply to the wardens' ultimatum and they remained true to their promise. From 26 January, Darwin was without a formal, trained Civil Defence organisation. Needless to say, an unofficial cadre remained.

The situation prevailing within the three Services in Darwin was different, reflecting the varying degree of priorities and impact of the war. In the early days of the war, the Navy had had greater involvement than the airmen of Darwin, who had experienced some warlike activity, while the Army had experienced none.

Three of the ships lying in the harbour on 14 February had seen significant action already. On 4 February, the USS *Houston* had been part of a US/Dutch fleet attempting to interfere with Japanese landings in the Flores Sea, when she was bombed. Despite the brilliant seamanship and evasive action of her skipper, Captain Rooks, a bomb hit number three main gun turret, killing 48 sailors and wounding 50. Once again, the Japanese would report the destruction of USS *Houston,* an occasion now so frequent that she was nicknamed the 'Galloping Ghost'. But, here she was arriving on the 14th in Darwin harbour, albeit with one inoperative gun turret.

The 22 year old 4-stack destroyer, USS *Peary,* had good cause to be regarded as a jinxed ship. She was a venerable lady, but it was not until 13 December that she was to see her first active service, after which followed an intense but short period of action. While tied to the wharf of the Cavite Naval Yard in the Philippines, she was struck by a Japanese bomb which killed eight and wounded a number of the crew, among whom was the Captain. She suffered a second attack on 26 December and put to sea two days later under the command of Lieutenant Commander Bermingham. While passing through the Macascar Strait, she was bombed and damaged by three Hudson aircraft of 2 Squadron RAAF. Her radio had become unserviceable and she was therefore unable to warn her attackers off. The very next morning, she was bombed and torpedoed by Japanese aircraft. Her arrival in Darwin harbour on 3 January and tasking for convoy escort had been a welcome respite, but for her, sadly, it was but the lull before the storm, and disaster.

The other veteran was a RAN Corvette, HMAS *Deloraine,* now immobilised in Darwin harbour while undergoing a refit. She had depth-charged and sunk a Japanese minelaying submarine, off Bathurst Island on 23 January.

* * *

Major-General D V J Blake commanded the Australian Land Forces from his Seventh Military District Headquarters in Larrakeyah Barracks. This was a recently-built camp, named after the local aboriginal tribe. It was well laid out, and closely resembled the equally-new and adjoining civil hospital. The General's order of battle included two infantry brigades whose forward positions would have been vulnerable to outflanking movements. The Australian forces' perennial weakness in armour was again confirmed by the absence of armoured units. There was, however, a proliferation of gunners, living up to their motto, 'Ubique'.* In a subsequent re-organisation, Darwin town was lightly held by fortress troops and two, later three, brigades, were deployed to camps down the Stuart Highway. In that way, General Blake argued, 'I could dispose my force so that I will be able to deal in time with the enemy's most probable course (simultaneous landings at Shoal and Byno Bays), at the same time taking the minimal risk, in case he does the unexpected, by keeping my whole force on the main road for rapid movement in any direction'.

The Coast Defence Artillery had six- and four-inch guns deployed to four positions, yet they would play no significant part in this story. Today, however, former members of the Royal Australian Artillery (RAA) have opened a War Museum in cramped accommodation in blockhouses, watch-towers, and the old command post. It almost seems that without this initiative, there would be no record of the fateful events which occurred on 19 February 1942.

American field artillery had been integrated with that of the RAA throughout the force. The only anti-aircraft guns, including a supporting Searchlight Company, were two batteries of 3.7 inch guns. The ten static guns were too few to cover the key areas and, in consequence, their effectiveness was diluted by dispersal. As heavy guns they were, of course, designed to engage high-flying targets. They were useless against the low-level attack now known to be favoured by the Japanese Zero. The most suitable gun to counter the fighters' ground attack was the 40 millimetre Bofors, but of these the ground forces had none. The guns had been sent to Malaya and Singapore, and General Blake's request for these guns had been unfruitful. At the time, Darwin was regarded only as a refuelling base. Soldiers and airmen would have to use .303 rifles and light machine-guns to engage the Zero – and would suffer the retaliatory consequences.

---

* 'Everywhere'.

Ammunition for the heavy anti-aircraft guns was in short supply and, in consequence, crews were poorly-trained. Some detachments even lacked fire-control instruments. The arrival of this vital equipment only just preceded that of the Japanese, but it meant that some of the anti-aircraft gunners fired their guns for the first time in earnest. In consequence, some rounds were seen to be exploding as much as 100 metres below their targets. As Commander Fuchida, the Japanese air commander would later confirm, 'anti-aircraft fire was intense but largely ineffectual'.

Such negligence understandably fostered low morale. Some soldiers had been in Darwin for two years, suffering the rigours of a physically and mentally taxing climate for the second time around as well as having to endure the enforced isolation. Some succumbed to the heat, loneliness and isolation and went 'troppo'*, requiring their evacuation to more temperate and populous climes. At the time of the Japanese attack, the Curtin government was in the process of investigating ways of rotating the troops in Darwin as a means of solving the problems of boredom and poor morale.

The last months of 1941 in Darwin had been marked by rioting and severe disorder, principally by disgruntled AIF men allegedly encouraged by the North Australia Workers' Union. The Military Board's solution of granting the regular soldiers six weeks' home leave proved insufficient. 'We've been trained, for 15 months and we want to go overseas, but all they give us is six weeks' leave. We will get overseas even if it means deserting when the home leave comes off and re-enlisting under false names.' The main source of the AIF's discontent was their conviction that they were being asked to carry out a function more suited to the militia. The fact was that the sum of Darwin's acceptable indigenous manpower had proved unable to fill the bill. Exceptionally, coloureds had been recruited for guard duties. They became known as the 'Black Watch'. To make up the shortfall, militia reinforcements had to be drawn from the southern states. Gavin Long described how New South Wales soldiers were selected for Darwin service according to the length of their crime sheets and how single officers were obliged to draw lots out of a hat. One of which had written on it a word which throughout Australia had become synonymous with an unique notoriety, 'Darwin'.

The privileges afforded the AIF also caused resentment among the RAN lower ranks. They had not gone on a rampage and therefore

---

* Tropical neurasthenia.

were not appeased by the reward of six weeks' home leave. The militia were equally unimpressed by the unruly behaviour of the truculent volunteers. What they thought of the AIF, however, was a matter of monumental insignificance. To the volunteer soldier of the AIF, relishing active service in foreign lands, the home-tied militiaman was held in varying degrees of disdain. They were labelled by the collective term 'chocos' – chocolate soldiers. For these men of the militia, wiring beaches over the Christmas period 1941, separated to all intents and purposes from their nearby families, came the realisation that they might just as well be abroad. For those who did volunteer to join the AIF, the prospect of refusal was certain because they were engaged in key posts.

Despite problems with the Navy and Army, their men were at least trained to be sailors or soldiers first and tradesmen second. The tradition of both Services and the *esprit de corps* that existed within ships or units were essential harmonising bonds. The Royal Australian Air Force, however, was in its infancy, barely having had time to establish habits, let alone traditions. They were not at all well placed to cope with the rapid expansion of the air arm, which had grown from 5,000 to 20,000 between 1939 and early 1942. It was, therefore, an arm of pilots and tradesmen lacking leadership, regimental training and staff duties.

The most alarming indictment of the Air Force was reflected in the total absence of a fighter. It was not that the Air Force had not recognised the need or had been short of offers. They had stuck to tradition, insisting that they wanted the British Beaufighter and were prepared to wait rather than accept the immediate offers of assistance emanating from North America. In fact, the RAAF did not receive the Beaufighter but instead took early delivery of Spitfires. These were to be flown with varying degrees of success. At 10.30 on 2 May 1943, the Japanese launched another of their frequent raids on the Darwin RAAF airbase. They lost 11 bombers and five Zeros but, of the 32 Spitfires scrambled, 15 did not return. When it was discovered that five of the aircraft had run out of fuel and that others had been lost due to sheer inexperience, the news was censored on the personal direction of Prime Minister Curtin.

Meanwhile, the Air Force employed licence-built T-6s, a general-purpose aircraft known in Australia as the Wirraway, as a fighter. On 20 January at Rabaul, seven Wirraways took on 120 carrier aircraft of Vice-Admiral Nagumo's First Air Fleet – Zeros with a top speed of 560 kilometres per hour. It was a pointless gesture. A signal, 'Nos Morituri

Te Salutamus'*, originated from Rabaul destined for the Air Board. As a result, the originator, Wing-Commander J M Lerew, was transferred.

The signal had served its purpose. A speedily-issued order confined the slow 330 kilometres per hour Wirraway to dive-bombing duties. Unfortunately, the Wirraway did not have the range to indulge in useful off-shore dive-bomb duties and, in the absence of suitable targets on the mainland, was relegated to in-shore reconnaissance. That is, of course, those aircraft which had the spares-backing to keep them in the air. Of the five Wirraways at Darwin on that fateful February day, not one was airworthy. Nine Wirraways had been dispersed 100 kilometres to the south at Batchelor field but, in the absence of communications, they could not be called forward when needed.

So it was that the North Western Area, based on Darwin, was entirely without Australian fighter support. Within the Area's establishment were 17 modern, but temperamental, Pratt and Whitney engined Hudson bombers. Six uncrewed airframes, were 500 kilometres to the south at Daly Waters. Six of the remaining 11 arrived early on the morning of 19 February, carrying standing refugees from Timor. Their arrival had been distinguished by having been engaged by the RAA anti-aircraft detachment at Fannie Bay while on their final approach to the airfield.

The command structure at RAAF Darwin was both confused and confusing. It was heavy on command, light on aircraft. The Commander North West Area, Air-Commodore D E L Wilson, superimposed his headquarters on that of the Station Commander, Wing-Commander Sturt Griffith. Not only that, but Wilson and some of his staff had taken rooms in Griffith's married quarter. Griffith lacked the freedom of command that he should have enjoyed. He had only been appointed Station Commander on 1 February, having been called up from his law firm in September 1939. He was not, therefore, a highly experienced officer. Nevertheless, he was sufficiently astute to deplore the poor morale that he found on the station as well as the high incidence of tropical sickness and sheer lack of interest. He resented the proximity of his superior's headquarters, which he saw as a mere duplication of his own responsibilities. In his operations building, he also provided a home for a Joint Service Headquarters, whose *raison d'être* was to co-ordinate the activities of all three Services.

---

* 'We who are about to die salute you'.

At about roughly the same time that Griffith assumed his command in Darwin, a former commander of a RAAF airbase in the Middle-East transited through the base. So mortified was he at the state of the station and its unpreparedness that he made a personal report to Wing-Commander Gerard Packer, Director of Air Intelligence. It was not the known shortage of fighter aircraft or the absence of a credible dual-structured anti-aircraft gun defence which had struck the visitor – it was recognised that these shortcomings could not be quickly overcome. What struck home was the apparent lack of awareness and urgency. Aircraft were grouped together for administrative convenience, the warning system was ineffective (a radar had been located at nearby Dripstone Caves but it did not have an antenna) and little attempt had been made to camouflage buildings and facilities.

The errors were not always on Darwin's side. Wilson had recognised the limitations of the Wirraways in the forward areas and ordered them to Daly Waters where, as we have seen, a reserve of Hudson bombers had also been deployed. When the Deputy Chief of the Air Staff heard of this move, he overruled Wilson and ordered the planes back to Darwin. Here they would all be destroyed on the ground. It appeared that the Air Force was singularly incapable of delegating authority down to the level at which it should have been properly exercised.

Curtin's final capitulation to the pleas from General Brett to reinforce Timor had little to do with strategic or tactical logic, but rather with solidarity. With Australia now under pressure, the adage that it is unwise to reinforce disaster appeared supremely appropriate to the prevailing case of the Dutch East Indies. Yet with Britain, the traditional backbone of Australian defence policy, now bundled speedily and unceremoniously out of the region, it would have been impolitic not to have demonstrated some degree of support and acquiescence with the wishes of the United States, the new bedfellow.

It was with reluctance that Australia agreed to the despatch of a joint force to Koepang, Timor. A battalion of Australian pioneers, American gunners and a mixed bag of specialist units were embarked on four transports in the harbour. The naval escorts were to be USS *Houston* and *Peary* and two RAN sloops, HMAS *Swan* and *Warrego*. Unfortunately, there was no air cover available to accompany the convoy.

There were only two American P-40 Kittyhawks in Darwin at the time the convoy was being assembled. Their pilots were Lieutenants

Robert G Oestreicher and Robert J Buel. Both aircraft were the unserviceable residue of the Third Pursuit Squadron which had been moved to Java. Reinforcement aircraft had been called forward and were patiently awaited, but after the convoy had been delayed for two days, the order for the ships to sail was given. The Senior Naval Officer Darwin justified his decision on the rational grounds that if the convoy had not left when it did, its destination could well have been in enemy hands. It was, therefore, with much apprehension that the convoy slipped anchor just after midnight on 15 February. A light drizzle was falling as the ships moved out towards the harbour entrance and the open sea.

On the same day that the convoy left Darwin, the unannounced arrival of the convoy's delayed escort squadron, under command of Major Floyd Pell, caused consternation which later gave way to relief. Pell had earlier been on MacArthur's air staff and had been instrumental in selecting Darwin as a stopover airfield for US air operations in the region. Events would show what a fateful decision that had been. The P-40s had flown across the continent. Of the 25 aircraft of the Thirty-Third Squadron, only ten reached Darwin. Pell's pilots were young, inexperienced and exhausted. Even if they had not been tired, their aircraft required urgent maintenance and the mechanics were not due to arrive until the next day.

The sea convoy's progress was monitored throughout the day by, amongst others, a Japanese Mavis Kawanishi flying-boat, maintaining a safe distance. *Houston* radioed through to Darwin for air support. Oestreicher was flying somewhere to the south and could not be raised. Buel's P-40 was now serviceable and he took off for the Timor Sea to intercept the flying-boat. After making contact, both aircraft shot one another down. Buel died and, of the Kawanishi's crew, there were five survivors who were interned. Occasionally, USS *Houston* would engage the enemy at long range, causing them to drop their bombs harmlessly. The Japanese were quite content to play along with this waiting game, both in order to confirm that the convoy was destined for Timor and also to allow it to sail beyond the radius of what they knew to be its improbable air support. Three hours after the initial contact report was heard in Darwin, the Senior Naval Officer there recommended that the convoy should return. The advice was not heeded because, now on the open sea, the ships were under the orders of Wavell's ABDA Headquarters in Java.

Just before mid-day on 16 February, the anticipated Japanese air attack of 35 bombers and nine flying-boats was launched at the convoy. USS *Houston* drew most of the attention upon herself by moving away from the other ships. Yet again, she demonstrated superb seamanship in avoiding countless bombs and by throwing up a wall of fire which served to keep the Japanese aircraft at high altitude. The ships in the convoy went on to survive a number of near misses, although two sailors were wounded, one mortally.

Now that the convoy had been detected and engaged, with her intentions so obvious, it would have been the height of folly to permit the mission to continue. Captain Rooks signalled ABDA Headquarters, recommending that his further progress should be aborted and suggesting that he be allowed to escort the convoy back to Darwin. There was a delay of two hours while the ABDA staff sought out Wavell, who gave his personal approval. The ships turned about, taking a direct course for Port Darwin, still 650 kilometres distant. All the while, the Allied ships were shadowed by Japanese aircraft.

For those in the town, the return of the battered convoy to Darwin on 18 February with its mission unaccomplished was ominous. A deep sense of foreboding prevailed among civilians and military alike. 'The return of the convoy confirmed my opinion that it would not be long before Darwin's turn came', said Abbott. For the Senior Naval Officer, Captain Thomas, the return of the convoy brought both relief and apprehension. 'They know where the bunny is now and they will be here soon enough to finish it off.' To be more precise, Thomas had confided in Group Captain Scherger on 18 February that 'we should have visitors' the following day, to which Scherger allegedly agreed. Thomas explained to the Royal Commission 'it is very obvious, is it not?' The closely-packed anchorages at Darwin had caused consternation among USN personnel arriving from the south. The mystery is why Thomas, if he was so convinced that an attack would occur on the 19th, did not either disperse the fleet lying at anchor or de-congest the bottleneck at the wharf. Evidence given before the Royal Commission also suggests that Thomas was told of the air armada spotted over Bathurst Island and heading south. Whatever his thought processes may have been, on the day, he got it badly wrong. In that, he was not alone.

With no further justification to remain in Darwin, USS *Houston* and *Peary* immediately refuelled and headed back out to the open sea, away from Darwin's vulnerable and congested anchorage. That night, the American ships were to encounter a Japanese submarine. This, USS *Peary* engaged with a series of depth-charges. When the action was broken off, the destroyer had consumed a substantial amount of oil; so much so that she had to separate from *Houston* and return to Darwin to refuel. She arrived back in the port at 1.00 am on Thursday 19 February.

Japanese Intelligence in Darwin was not as well-developed as it had been in Hawaii. Not surprisingly, Darwin was not so important a target and, at the outbreak of war, the authorities had been quick to round up the Japanese employed, chiefly, in the pearling trade. That fellow-travellers did still exist in Darwin was unquestionable. An officer aboard the *Zealandia* in the harbour observed a person signalling with a flashlight to distant aircraft out to sea. The officer logged the occurrence but thought no more of it until forcibly reminded later. Over the following days, the authorities twice apprehended the same man signalling messages seaward. He was an Italian. Among the 281 aliens registered by military intelligence in the town on 11 June 1940, 21 were Italian. After Italy entered the war, and after due processing, only one third were detained. The internment rules were very loosely interpreted and applied by Abbott.

The aircraft spotted on 18 February from *Zealandia* were reconnaissance aircraft from Admiral Nagumo's flagship, the *Akagi*. It had been from *Akagi* (Red Castle) that the attack on Pearl Harbor was launched. On 18 February, she led her carrier taskforce undetected into the Timor Sea. Among the 16 ships in the Group were the same key personalities who had wrought havoc upon Hawaii.

The 36,000-ton, 28 knot *Akagi* had been converted from a battle-cruiser in the 1930s and given a full-length steel flight-deck. With her in the First Carrier Division was *Kaga* (Increased Joy). *Kaga* was originally laid down as a battleship, but she was later converted to a carrier within the margins permitted by the Washington Naval Limitation Treaty. It was the commander of the Second Carrier Division, Rear-Admiral Yamaguchi, who had recommended the initiation of the existing plan to attack Darwin. His proposition was made at the time the First Carrier Division was attacking Rabaul, the clear inference being that the task was within the capability of his two carriers.

The Yamaguchi initiative came at a time when the Japanese naval staff were undecided whether to attack next at Darwin or to go further afield to Ceylon. When Commander Genda, the architect of the raid on Pearl Harbor was consulted, he opted for Darwin which he identified as the more immediate threat to Japanese intentions in Java.

Admiral Yamamoto had led a minority group in favour of an amphibious landing and invasion of Darwin. A larger group argued that although the town was only lightly held, an invasion would tie up too many troops. This group successfully maintained that the same effect would be achieved by sustained, accurate bombing. Yamamoto acceded to the later view and on 31 January gave clearance for the attack on Darwin but, always cautious, he assigned both the First and Second Carrier Divisions to the mission. Overall command fell, therefore, not to the thrusting Yamaguchi but to Nagumo. Yamaguchi was annoyed but philosophical. In his group he had two modern, 30 knot light carriers which had been completed in 1938. They were his flagship, *Soryu* (Green Dragon), and *Hiryu* (Flying Dragon).

Also included in the Japanese Carrier Force were four modern 35 knot, 12,000-ton, eight-inch gun cruisers, *Tone*, *Chikuma*, *Maya* and *Takao*. All four had been built in contravention of the Washington Naval Limitation Treaty. The supreme irony was that not too far distant in the same theatre was the hybrid British heavy cruiser, HMS *Exeter*. Finally, as eyes and ears to the Japanese group, came a nine-destroyer screen.

The decision to attack Darwin on Thursday 19 February had been made as early as 9 February. It was planned to invade Timor on 20 February, hence the necessity of neutralising Darwin before that attack could begin. In orders circulated to the carrier fleet on that day was an emphatic mission:

> At an opportune time, the carrier task forces will conduct mobile warfare, first in the Arafura Sea and next in the Indian Ocean, endeavouring to annihilate the enemy strength in the Port Darwin area and to intercept and destroy enemy naval and transport fleets, at the same time attacking enemy strength in the Java area from behind.

In compliance with these orders, Commander Genda planned a two-phased air attack. The first would consist of a strike by 188 carrier-borne aircraft, namely, 36 Zero fighters, 71 dive-bombers and 81 level-bombers. The follow-up second phase strike was to be launched by 51 bombers from the recently captured airfields in the Dutch East Indies.

The leader of the carrier-borne air group was Commander Mitsuo Fuchida, exponent of the superiority of air power and the same man who led the air-raid on Pearl Harbor. Sitting in his three-seater Kate level-bomber, he was ready once more to take off from *Akagi* under Nagumo's watchful eye. The weather forecast was favourable and, when 365 kilometres north-west of Darwin, Nagumo ordered his force to turn into the prevailing, monsoon-bearing, north-west wind. The carriers were now sailing away from Darwin and would maintain that course after reducing speed once all the aircraft had left. For the moment, it was necessary to increase speed in order to raise the wind velocity over the decks to 42 kilometres per hour. First, a squadron of Zeros took off to cover the launching of the bombers, which proceeded according to plan until all 188 aircraft had taken up their positions at cruising altitude. It was 8.45 am when Fuchida wheeled his air armada round onto a course of 148 degrees. In just over an hour's time they would be over Darwin.

* * *

Darwin's radar equipment, one of only three sets in Australia, was not operational on 19 February. It was still in the process of being installed. There were, however, other active sources of intelligence and early-warning available. The Australian Consul in Portuguese Timor gave RAAF Darwin two to three day's warning of the build-up of Japanese air movement in the region, including a report of the presence of an aircraft carrier. Instead of the operations staff taking immediate precautions, the RAAF Intelligence staff first set about the analysis and validation of the data.

A further source of information was a group of dedicated volunteer coast-watchers, first established in 1927 by the Department of Defence. These were men whose normal employment took them to remote parts of the coastline and islands from where, in the course of their daily duties, they could observe and report movements of ships and aircraft. For communication purposes they were issued, more often than not, with pedal-operated radios, and reported-in to larger radio stations in the more populated areas. The coast-watcher on the northern tip of Melville Island was John Gribble, and 80 kilometres to his south was another coast-watcher, Father John McGrath at the Roman Catholic Mission on Bathurst Island, 80 kilometres north of Darwin. The inhabitants of both islands were well aware that if an attack on Darwin was scheduled, it made good strategic sense to account for Melville and Bathurst islands first. The threat served to concentrate both the minds and the level of alertness of the observers.

At 9.15 am on Thursday 19 February, the duty Warrant-Officer at HMAS *Coonawarra* radio station picked up a signal from Gribble reporting the sighting of a large number of aircraft. The Warrant-Officer immediately contacted the Senior Naval Intelligence Officer who, in turn, relayed the message to RAAF Intelligence. The intelligence staff were able to argue away what Gribble had reported, as being the ten P-40s of Major Pell's Squadron, tasked that morning to deploy to Java. The time-and-space equation, however, was all wrong. Pell did not take off from Darwin until 9.15 am, and therefore could not have been over Melville Island. Moreover, if it had been Pell's squadron, he was well off-course for a Java destination; an error which would have been most improbable, since a B-17 had been specifically assigned to navigate Pell to Java. Nor could it have been Pell's flight returning, because it had long been the practice for aircraft to return to base on the backbearing of their outward leg.

Darwin had suffered a number of false alarms air-attacks. Civilian humour and morale was fading every time they were turned out onto the hot, humid, fly- and mosquito-infested beaches, or the ovens cut into the ground called trenches, only to find that nothing had happened. After successive anti-climaxes and witch-hunts, a great reluctance had developed to initiate an air-attack alert.

Meanwhile, Fuchida's air contingent had passed over Gribble's location and was flying in formation to the north-west of the Sacred Heart Mission on Bathurst Island. At 9.30 am, the distant roar of engines caused the Mission's Aborigines to look skyward. They saw more aircraft than they had ever seen before. Father McGrath instantly recognised the portents contained in this sighting and, while rushing to his radio, gave concurrent orders to evacuate the village and Mission.

The priest turned his dial to an emergency frequency which should give him direct contact with Darwin Radio, call-sign VID. The roar outside was deafening as the aircraft continued their journey southward. McGrath reflected that if he could get his message through, the inhabitants of Darwin would have 20 minutes' warning. 'Eight SE to VID', called Father McGrath in clear and going straight to the meat of his transmission. 'I have an urgent message. An unusually large formation bearing down on us from the north-west. Identity suspect. Visibility not clear. Over.'

McGrath was relieved to receive an immediate acknowledgement from the Darwin operator. 'Eight SE from VID. Message received. Stand by.' An incoming flight of Zeros with chattering machine-guns forced McGrath to leave his set and take cover. When he returned to his radio, the smoke from a burning American Beechcraft drifted through the air. Try as he might, McGrath could not raise Darwin again. Japanese electronic counter-measures had effectively jammed his frequency. Theoretically, they had been too late. A more relaxed and thankful clergyman returned to his duties, grateful that his message had been acknowledged.

It was 9.37 am when the Darwin radio operator received a 'Roger'* after relaying McGrath's message to RAAF Operations. The initial assessment of those present was that it was probably Pell's P-40s. Apparently no one thought to contact United States Air Force (USAF) Operations to obtain a location report from Pell's B-17. The report of activity over Bathurst Island, the jamming of McGrath's frequency following on from Gribble's report and, coming so soon after the sea convoy's failure to reach Java, should have been sufficient justification to suspect that something out of the ordinary was happening.

McGrath's message landed on the Station Commander's desk. Griffith was told that the message had also been passed to North West Area and the Joint or Area Command Headquarters. The Wing-Commander assumed that the executive decision would be made at his superior headquarters. The Commander of North West Area, however, had taken himself off to ABDA Headquarters in Java, returning to Broome on 19 February, where he was obliged to wait two days until an aircraft became available. His deputy, Group Captain Scherger, was away from the base attending to a VIP. Meanwhile, RAAF Operations, alone responsible for the positive identification of the aircraft, dallied.

In order to achieve complete surprise, Genda's tactic was to fly to the east of Darwin and then turn, to make an indirect approach from the south-east. This was a calculated risk, for it could confirm Japanese intentions and increase the vigilance and preparedness of the defenders.

At 9.46 am, a battery commander stationed at Nightcliff, 11 kilometres north of Darwin, was watching aircraft weaving patterns in the sky above him. When he saw one, a P-40, crash into the sea in flames and a parachute subsequently develop from where the plane's descent had begun, he telephoned RAAF Operations with his report. The response, 'If this is a raid we know nothing of it', was staggeringly glib. The Major then rang Army Headquarters, but also to no avail.

On 18 February, Major Pell received orders to fly his squadron to Java, thereby denuding Darwin of its fighter cover. The American air-

---

* 'Message received and understood'.

craft did not come under the command of North West Area, so although the local Australian commanders were dismayed by the decision, there was nothing that they could do. The flight schedule required Pell's ten P-40s, plus Darwin's one remaining P-40 now under Pell's command, to take off at dawn on 19 February. Already, intelligence reports were painting an extremely pessimistic picture of the situation in Java. Even if the P-40s survived the attention of the hordes of Zeros, it could well be that they would not find a friendly airfield on which to land.

When dawn came, the squadron had not taken off. Pell's own air-craft had developed a fault in its cooling system and the other ten aircraft were held-over until repairs could be effected. As time marched on, Pell decided to take a subordinate's plane, finally taking all ten remaining aircraft aloft at 9.15 am.

Fifteen minutes into his journey, with radio contact with Koepang lost, USAAF Operations advised Pell that the weather ahead of him was deteriorating. Pell considered his situation. With the exception of Lieutenant Oestreicher, the pilot he inherited in Darwin, the other eight pilots were absolutely raw and half-trained. None had ever flown a combat mission, nor had they flown in bad weather con-ditions. Perhaps Pell was looking for an excuse to abort a mission which appeared impossible. Indeed, he was encouraged to do so by USAAF Operations and that is what he did.

On arrival back over the airfield at Darwin, Pell took half the squadron down with him to land, and ordered Oestreicher to patrol with the other half at 5,000 metres for two hours. Oestreicher led the other four planes in his flight in pairs up towards the assigned alti-tude. Below them was Darwin harbour, in which the close-packed shipping was clearly visible.

As Commander Fuchida brought his aircraft around from their cir-cuitous route to line them up on the 45 ships below him, he was amazed to discover that the element of surprise had been so com-plete. Servicemen in and around the harbour had not been stood-to, and civilians could be seen going about their normal business. His targets were clearly identifiable, the agreed priorities being first the warships, then the merchant ships, followed by the docks' facilities. 'The harbour', he recalled, 'was crowded with all kinds of ships which we picked off at our leisure'.

The level-bombers closed on their victims with bomb-doors open. There was no defensive fire. The alarm was raised by the elderly RAN Depot Ship ('nothing more than a floating workshop'), HMAS

Platypus, just as the first bombs were being released. The time was 9.58 am.

USS *Peary* had still not refuelled when Lieutenant-Commander Bermingham first spotted the Japanese dive-bombers. At first they were mistaken for the anticipated US air reinforcements. When the mistake was recognised, Bermingham ordered his ship immediately to weigh anchor and make for the open sea. Guns were hurriedly manned as the ship's crew worked feverishly to pull on board over 75 fathoms of anchor chain. That done, the *Peary* began to accelerate towards the harbour mouth. Fuchida's high-flying level-bombers, however, were equal to the task, displaying unbelievable accuracy against the moving targets below them. The 1,900-ton *Peary* was struck by five bombs. The ship had not achieved sufficient speed to avoid them. She was further slowed in her attempt to escape by successive bomb strikes and began to settle by the stern while still maintaining some forward momentum. She had already taken on board the bomb which would destroy her – a delayed-action one which had entered the magazine. When the bomb detonated, the ship disintegrated in a sea of flame and smoke. The gunners were still firing the fo'c's'le gun until her bow pointed in the air and then slipped below the surface of the oily black sea. Lieutenant-Commander Bermingham and 79 of his ship's company were lost. 52 men survived.

The 1,190-ton USS *William B. Preston* got underway at the same time as the ill-fated *Peary*. The *William B. Preston* had been in Darwin since January, employed as a tender to the US Catalina seaplanes. In her holds was a substantial quantity of aviation fuel. A bomb hit her stern, killing four of the crew and starting a fire. The Captain put up a smokescreen as he zig-zagged across the harbour, dodging bombs, but almost colliding with a number of ships still at anchor. The Japanese did not follow-up their attack on the tender, possibly in the mistaken belief that the volume of smoke and erratic course were the death-throes of a doomed ship. Doomed she was not. She was later to reach Broome, Western Australia, without further incident.

The largest ship in the harbour was the 12,566-ton USS *Meigs*. She and the other three troopers which had made the profitless journey towards Timor were the next to attract the bombers' attention. The *Meigs* did not last long. She received several direct hits from dive-bombers, was soon ablaze and sank, taking with her two of her crew. The USS *Mauna Loa* had her hatches open when the attack occurred. Two bombs went through the open hatches, breaking the ship's back and setting her on fire. Five crew members were killed. The USS *Port Mar* was machine-gunned and, with hull holed, beached alongside the Australian coastal trader *Turagi*.

The British-registered *British Motorist*, 6,891-tons, and the 3,289-ton US freighter *Admiral Halstead*, had both arrived in Darwin to replenish the diminishing oil and fuel stocks. The first bomb to hit the British ship struck the bridge area, killing the Captain and a wireless operator. The ship was already well on fire when a second bomb hit the bow, adding to the already substantial conflagration. Crewmen leapt overboard to escape the flames, only to be confronted by blazing oil on the sea surface. Many survived due to the quick action of the minesweeper HMAS *Tolga*. As the burnt and half-drowned survivors were pulled out of the blazing morass, the list of their former ship accentuated to port until she capsized and sank.

The *Admiral Halstead* was doubly fortunate. She was damaged by a near miss. Her Captain took the wise precaution of jettisoning his cargo of 44-gallon drums of petrol, which floated harmlessly ashore. From that point, the *Admiral Halstead* received no further attention from the Japanese aircraft. This was just as well, for the records suggest that other than the Captain and a solitary sailor, the remainder of the crew deserted.

At the time that the attack began, no fewer than three ships were tied up to Darwin's problem wharf. Both *Neptuna* and *Barossa* were damaged in the initial onslaught, which also destroyed part of the jetty killing a number of wharfies. Both ships, however, were immobilised by other ships tied alongside on the seaward side. HMAS *Swan* was quick to cast off from *Neptuna*, but not quick enough to avoid a near miss which killed three of her crew and wounded 22 others. *Barossa* was hemmed in by a naval lighter and appeared destined to remain where she was for the duration of the attack. The irony of it all, with the wharf being progressively destroyed by successive attacks, was the nature of *Barossa*'s cargo; piles for the proposed, new, improved Darwin wharf.

The cargo aboard the 5,932-ton *Neptuna* however was lethal. She was unarguably the most dangerous ship in the harbour, laden with high explosives and depth charges. In the mistaken belief that she would be riding at anchor for a few days, the Australian owners of the passenger ship had permitted one of her engines to be overhauled. She had already been waiting a week to be unloaded, so that when her turn eventually came to have her cargo discharged, she had not been prepared to miss the opportunity. She had manoeuvred herself into the jetty but, due to the scheduled repairs, would be unable to leave under her own steam.

The first dive-bomber to hit *Neptuna* came out of a cloud. The bomb tore through the bridge, landing in the saloon where a large proportion of the crew were taking shelter. A second bomb tore into the engine room. Soon the ship was alight from stem to stern. With the jetty cut, the crew had to jump overboard into a sea of fuel oil, patches of which were ablaze. Some of the non-swimming Chinese appeared to prefer the danger of the fire, now raging out of control on board, to the leap over the side into the smouldering sea. Some were hurled overboard by other crew members.

Almost everyone in the harbour that day was aware of the danger that could be expected if *Neptuna* blew up. She held the attention of men near and far, as though one eye was on the blazing *Neptuna* while the other kept watch for the Japanese. Gradually, the ship's plates turned to a glowing red, as if to announce the imminence of the massive explosion which followed. Smoke and flames leapt 100 metres into the sky. The whole town shook, and men and ships over a wide radius were showered by debris. Above the place where the ship was berthed, a massive mushroom of smoke ballooned upwards into the air. 'Black smoke was shot with flames as it rose', wrote Abbott, who had watched the ship's destruction from Government House.

> The ship was blown in halves. The stern and engines sank alongside the wharf. The bow floated for a few minutes, and then turned on its side and also sank. One piece of her side-plating containing two portholes with the glass intact was found 300 yards away.

Forty-five members of the crew, including the Captain, perished.

The state of mind of those aboard *Barossa* immediately prior to *Neptuna*'s detonation can be imagined. The naval tug *Wato* sailed in to tow away the lighter which had secured *Barossa* as an involuntary prisoner to the jetty. No sooner had a line been put aboard *Barossa* than *Neptuna* went up. The blast passed over *Barossa* and *Wato*, so neither capsized, but *Barossa* caught fire. The flames were to be extinguished by the crew of the busy HMAS *Tolga* which succeeded in dragging *Barossa* away from the wharf.

Another ship to feel the sense of vulnerability acutely was the Corvette, HMAS *Katoomba*. She was in the floating dock being repaired after a collision with an American tanker. She was defended with a great deal of enthusiasm, but in reality the Japanese could have sunk both her and the dock in which she now found herself involuntarily suspended. The bombers had, after all, a limited number of bombs and an unlimited number of targets.

Zealandia was one of the Australian coastal traders requisitioned into service. She was a most unfortunate ship. She had arrived in Darwin on 6 February and now, on 19 February, had only been part-unloaded. She was rocked by two explosions, sinking very quickly with only her masts protruding above the water.

Not all the ships were unlucky. HMAS *Platypus* had been fortunate to have been near-missed on three occasions, the closest of the bombs falling by the stern but failing to explode. Captain and crew were later subject to criticism for going ashore after the attack and remaining there during daylight hours. Luck, however, had not been kind to the hospital ship *Manunda*. She should not have been in Darwin in the first place. She had been en route to Singapore when the rapid military deterioration had caused her to be held-over at Darwin to await developments. The 9,115-ton Australian hospital ship, the second largest vessel in the harbour, survived the bombing runs of the level-bombers untouched, leading some to believe that her immunity was being respected. There was no doubt that she was clearly designated as a hospital ship, with red crosses painted prominently on funnels and decks. The dive-bombers that followed did not heed the international symbols, and released two bombs at her. Twelve of those on board were killed, but this did not prevent the surviving crew members from receiving wounded and sick from the harbour area and ashore. With 266 patients on board, she weighed anchor at 11.30 pm on Friday 20 February, reaching Fremantle with no further difficulty.

Significantly, in the Russo-Japanese War, when the Russian hospital ship and the hospital at Port Arthur were hit by Japanese 11 inch shells, there was an international howl of protest. After the raid on Pearl Harbor, Commander Fuchida was summoned personally to report to the Emperor that no non-combatants and no hospital ships had been struck. Fuchida gave that guarantee.

It was the dive-bombers that had done the damage at Darwin. Perhaps it had been due to a combination of the release of adrenalin and over-zealousness. Some ground observers reported having seen Japanese pilots laughing with enjoyment as they indulged in their bombing and machine-gunning. The fact that the civilian hospital, also identified by large red crosses, was attacked, lends credence to a commonly-held view that many Japanese regarded hospitals as legitimate targets. Fuchida admitted having seen the red crosses on the hospital ship, but the dive-bomber pilots apparently told him that they had not.

The attack lasted 45 minutes; a minute for every ship in the harbour, for most had received some degree of attention. When it was over, eight ships had been sunk, four had run aground, and 11 were badly damaged. The majority of those killed in the raid, 160 out of an estimated 243, died on or among the ships in the harbour. Many of the sailors, and possibly some of the ships, particularly USS *Peary*, might have been saved if the warnings had been acted upon and the alert sounded. It was highly probable that *Neptuna* could have been towed away from the wharf to open water. At the time, the Japanese admitted the loss of two aircraft while Darwin's defenders claimed a tally of 23. The actual loss was probably seven aircraft.

The subsequent Royal Commission, convened to investigate and determine the truth of events that occurred at Darwin, found its efforts to identify what had gone wrong with the warning system frustrated by fabrication, apparent forgery, and absence of records. The efficiency of the Area Command Headquarters was impaired by petty jealousy, poor staff work, failure to pass information, and a fatal reluctance to make decisions. Members of all three Services sought to distance themselves from any blame for the indecision which had been so instrumental in maximising the disaster. None of the Service staffs was entirely blameless but, since the ultimate responsibility for identification lay with the RAAF, that is where most of the blame rested. There was always too much emphasis on the need for positive identification prior to a warning being given. This did not apply only to the RAAF. When an army sentry on Casurina Beach telephoned his brigade headquarters to say that a wave of Japanese aircraft had flown over, the cynical duty-officer asked the soldier how he knew that they were Japanese planes. 'Because', came back the reply, 'they have got bloody big red spots on'. To confirm the accuracy of the identification, the sound of falling bombs could be heard emanating from the harbour area.

Fuchida led his pilots back to the carriers. It had been, he would admit, 'a sledgehammer to crack a nut'. As a bonus, the jubilant Japanese came across two American supply ships, *Don Isidro* and *Florence D.* north-west of Bathurst Island. The *Don Isidro* was bombed and caught fire, but drifted ashore enabling most of the crew to make their escape. The *Florence D.* went to the bottom. Among the survivors from the *Florence D.* were the crew of a US Navy Catalina shot down earlier by nine inbound Zeros. They had been picked up by the sup-

ply ship after only 30 minutes in the water. When they found themselves again in the water after the *Florence D.* sank under them, they
made for Bathurst Island, from where they were picked up on 22
February by HMAS *Warrnambool*.

It was Melville Island, adjacent to Bathurst Island, which would
provide the first thread for the final part of the trilogy. One of
Fuchida's pilots from the *Hiryu*, Petty-Officer Hajime Toyoshima,
crash-landed his fighter there. Interrogators formed an opinion that
his heart had not been in the attack and his crash-landing had, therefore, not been accidental.

All trace of Toyoshima was lost. The record shows that the first prisoner-of-war captured on Australian soil and sent south, was not
Toyoshima, the fighter pilot but Tadao Minami, a Sergeant-Gunner
from a land-based bomber that allegedly caught fire on the way to
Darwin. A Japanese seaplane landed off Melville Island to collect the
downed fighter pilot, but could find no trace of him. Toyoshima did
not return to Japan after the war, nor did he die in a prisoner-of-war
camp. Circumstantial evidence points to Toyoshima having changed
his name to Tadao Minami, one of the first Japanese prisoners to
enter the Cowra prisoner-of-war camp. He was to prove a key figure
in the drama that would later occur at Cowra and is described in
Chapter 4.

Meanwhile, at the RAAF airbase minutes before the attack, Major
Pell had taxied to a quiet part of the airfield, where he took advantage of the shade under the wing of his aircraft. From his open cockpit he could hear the exchange of messages between Oestreicher's
flight somewhere in the sky above him.

Oestreicher was still climbing towards 5,000 metres when, just past
the half-way point, he saw a plane diving towards his flight from
above. He recognised the aircraft immediately. The red roundels on
the wings and fuselage merely confirmed his identification. 'Zeros,
Zeros, Zeros', he screamed into his radio. The P-40s were divided by
the suddenness of the attack, diving in different directions and jettisoning belly tanks. In minutes, two of the Kittyhawks had been shot
down.

Oestreicher pulled back his stick, climbing into the sun. As he surveyed the scene, he was amazed to see the mass of Zeros surrounding
him. He ordered the remaining pilots to climb up into the heavier
cloud to the south of Darwin. There was no response. Two pilots were
dead, one had crash-landed at the base, and another was the pilot on
the end of the parachute seen by the gunner Major at Nightcliff.

On the ground Pell was stung into action as he sensed the urgency in the voice coming through his radio. 'Zeros, Zeros, Zeros.' He ordered the mechanic to take the belly tanks off and told the four wide-eyed pilots to follow him. The first three aircraft bounced over the rough ground between the runways, heading into the wind to get airborne without delay. They were sitting ducks for the marauding Zeros. Pell had barely climbed to 30 metres when his plane blew up. He baled out, but the canopy did not have time to develop fully. He hit the ground with a thud. Only when he began to move did those watching jump out of their trenches to go to his assistance. It was to be a brave but useless gesture, for an incoming Zero tore Pell apart with cannon-shell as he lay on the ground still attached to his parachute. The second pilot behind Pell did not even get airborne, but slumped dead over his controls. The third plane managed to climb into the sky, and gamely engaged the Zeros before being shot down. The pilot baled out over the harbour and was rescued from the mangrove swamp by a motor boat.

The last two planes took off together, but one was very soon in trouble and the pilot got out. The Japanese fighters pounced with machine-guns blazing as he dangled from the end of his 'chute. The accompanying pilot, a Lieutenant Glover, saw his colleague's predicament and attacked the Zeros. One was seen to go down. Glover circled the defenceless pilot as he made his slow progress earthward. All the time, the Kittyhawk was taking punishment. At 1,000 metres, Glover's plane went into a steep dive, ending in a heavy pancake-landing on the airfield's perimeter. The aircraft turned over and over, scattering pieces around the base, until the main shell, essentially the engine and cockpit, came to rest. Amazingly, Glover stepped out. He had a nasty head-wound and staggered around, dazed and disorientated. He was saved from the Zeros' *coup de grace* by an Australian who pulled him to safety in the nick of time. The pilot on the parachute also survived.

Oestreicher wisely decided to stay aloft until the attack ended. For the most part, he stayed in cloud at 5,000 metres. It was at that altitude that he encountered and engaged two dive-bombers. Both planes hit the ground a kilometre apart, becoming the first allied air victories over Australia. Oestreicher the survivor returned to the RAAF base with his undercarriage damaged. His was the only fighter remotely capable of being repaired. Pell and half of his pilots had died in the space of 30 minutes, and all of Thirty-Three Squadron's aircraft had been destroyed. Yet to strike, however, was the Japanese land-based bomber force. An early victim of that bombing was to be Oestreicher's P-40.

Group Captain Scherger (later Air Chief Marshal Sir Frederick Scherger), the senior resident officer in Darwin on 19 February, had driven out of the airfield gate eight minutes before the first raid. He had an appointment with a visiting senior RAAF officer at the prestigious, recently-completed Hotel Darwin. The officer he was due to meet was Air Marshal Richard Williams, one of the driving forces in the development of Australia's fledgling air arm.

The Group Captain's car was mid-way between the town and the airfield when his thoughts were interrupted by the sound of anti-aircraft gunfire. He stopped, got out of his car, and saw the approaching Japanese air armada. Jumping back into his car, he turned around in the road and drove quickly to his Headquarters at the RAAF base. Scherger had been a former Darwin Station Commander, but was now the Senior Air Staff Officer to Air Commodore Wilson, absent on duty in Java.

As Sherger's car approached the gates, he ducked automatically as Glover's low-flying, damaged P-40 flew over, struggling to reach the runway. By the time the car reached the gate, the plane had crash-landed. The Group Captain took cover under a tree while the airfield was being systematically beaten-up by strafing Zeros and dive-bombers. In a lull, Scherger tried to reach his Headquarters, one of the few undamaged buildings on the base, but a driver had fled from his vehicle, leaving it abandoned in the gateway, blocking the entrance to the airfield.

The Zero and dive-bomber pilots had complete freedom to do as they wished over the airbase. The only opposition came from airmen armed with light and medium machine-guns and .303 rifles. One of the Vickers machine-guns was manned by Wing-Commander Archibald Tindal. He engaged the Zeros as they sped up and down the runway, until a cannon-shell struck him in the throat, killing him instantly. He was the first RAAF officer to be killed on active duty on Australian soil. An airfield to the south of Katherine was named after him.

There was a second, smaller airfield at Parap, used for civil flights and home for a flight of Wirraways. The field does not exist today, having been absorbed by the urban sprawl of modern Darwin. In its heyday, Parap had been an important field, principally because it was the landfall for the air pioneers flying in from the north. The first of many trail blazers were Ross and Keith Smith, who landed at Parap in

1919 in their Vickers Vimy after making the first England-Australia flight.

In February 1942, the field was quiet. The Wirraways were all unserviceable, and the Qantas Empire Airways* staff responsible for co-ordinating the Sydney-Singapore flying-boat service had recently lost that task due to a re-scheduling of the service through Broome. The most important function of the civil airfield lay in its radio communications.

The Department of Civil Aviation staff on duty had been alerted by the initial dogfight, which they witnessed over the sea to the north. In the absence of any alarm having been raised, a check was made with RAAF Operations by means of the teleprinter link. 'Is it all clear?', to which came the reply, 'All clear now'. Apparent reassurance was provided at that very moment by the sound of many aircraft approaching from the 'home side', the south. The civilian air staff believed they were watching a large flight of American aircraft, until the anti-aircraft fire disabused them of that idea. The radio operator tapped out on his morse keyboard the news that would spread throughout the continent, that Darwin was being attacked. Some acknowledgements had been received before the transmitters were shut down and the staff took cover from the bombs already falling on the airfield.

The bombing of the town of Darwin can be ascribed to over-zealousness. The targets given to the pilots were similar to those at Pearl Harbor; essentially military, shipping, and the wharf area. The town had not been included as a target. Most of the damage occurred within a tight radius of the wharf. To dismiss this as inaccurate bombing would be an underestimation of the skill of the Japanese pilots.

* * *

After the hospitals, the Post Office was the next largest employer of the residue of the women who had remained in Darwin. Abbott had urged the postmaster, 47 year old Hurtle Bald, to send his six female employees, among whom were Bald's wife and daughter, away to the safety of the south. Bald prevaricated.

The first sound of the bombing caused most of those working at the Post Office to seek shelter in the trench in the Balds' garden. The

---

* Qantas Empire Airways was an amalgamation of the British Imperial Airways and the original Australian company from which today's Qantas derives its name, Queensland and Northern Territory Air Services.

nine crouching occupants should have had reasonable confidence in the structure in which they found themselves. It had been carefully built and strengthened, but was not equal to the direct hit which killed instantly ten of the employees in the post office area. The postmaster's body was blown into a tree, and all the rescuers could do for the others was to cover the bodies, stripped of their clothing by the blast, with curtains torn down from shattered windows.

The nearby police barracks and government offices were also hit. A bomb had exploded over the road at Government House. One of the Administrator's servants was buried under a slab of concrete from the shattered offices, apparently killing her instantly.

Abbott's task, after the 'all clear' had been sounded at 10.40 am, was to organise the evacuation from Darwin. For that contingency, a number of key individuals clambered over the debris surrounding Government House to liaise and make the necessary plans. Above the house, the Australian flag was still flying as the drone of the Japanese planes disappeared to the north. It had taken on a dilapidated look, being damaged by bullets and bomb fragments. The large white star of the Southern Cross had disappeared, but the flag flew proudly in the breeze above the shattered little town, the first ever victim of offensive action against the Australian mainland.

* * *

As soon as the first attack was over, Group Captain Scherger moved quickly to his operations room, his fertile mind already contemplating revenge. His first thought was to send three of the surviving Hudsons to search for the carriers and, once located, the Hudsons would direct a back-up collection of Wirraways and A-24 dive-bombers from Batchelor to attack the Japanese. These thoughts were never to be converted into action because the landline between Darwin and Batchelor was down. That fact, and the destruction of the ground-to-air link which prevented the Hudsons from talking to Operations, saved the lives of a number of Batchelor's pilots. Had contact been made, there is little doubt that the Zeros would have made mincemeat of any hurriedly cobbled-together air intervention force.

Scherger remained unaware of the warnings received from the outlying islands until later in the evening. While he was trying desperately to master the situation, he had to brief Air Marshal Williams, who had made his own way to the airfield. In addition, another VIP,

American Air Force General Patrick Hurley, had arrived in a Liberator. All things considered, the RAAF base had not received as much attention as the harbour, the adjoining town, or the shipping. The airmen, however, had never been under fire before, and many were unnerved and visibly shaken.

The Group Captain was well into his briefing of the Air Marshal when, at 11.58 am, the lookout on board HMAS *Platypus* focused his binoculars on what at first appeared to be three high-flying birds approaching from the south-west. On closer examination, they proved to be three flights of nine bombers at an altitude of approximately 6,000 metres. Closing on that group from the opposite direction were a further 27 twin-engined Betty bombers from Ambon and the Celebes. There were no escorting fighters, for the Japanese knew that they would not be required. The orders given to the 54 bombers were precise and simple – destroy the RAAF airbase. While sailors and townsfolk braced themselves for a second attack, the bombers passed them by, drawn as though by a magnet to the military airfield.

Scherger and Williams were interrupted in their discussions by a staff officer, who warned them of the approaching aircraft. Both senior officers left the building together, jumping into a nearby trench which had been dug personally by Scherger. The bombs were already falling. General Hurley's Liberator was one of the first casualties as the two waves of aircraft converged on each other to release their loads.

The attack on the airfield lasted for 25 minutes and was as good an example of the effectiveness of pattern-bombing as could have been demonstrated. The pilot of a relief aircraft, flown up from Daly Waters to take General Hurley on to Sydney, said that it had been the most complete job of destruction that he had ever witnessed. Fortunately, only six further men on the base were killed, but the real damage was mental rather than physical.

Amidst the destruction and disarray resultant from two air attacks in as many hours, and with the warning system inoperable, the Station Commander, Wing-Commander Griffith, decided to evacuate the base. Rumours of the impending invasion were rife at the time Griffith made his decision, which was later to be described by Scherger as 'correct in concept'. If there was a fault, it lay in the dissemination of the order, not written, but passed by word-of-mouth on a casual basis, instructing airmen to go half a mile down the road, and then half a mile inland.

The combination of poor morale, bad leadership, indifferent training, and a message that became progressively distorted, were the ingredients which dropped the flag on what came to be known as the 'Adelaide River Stakes'. A large proportion of the airbase population panicked and took to their heels. Among that number were some of the men's officers. Once the seriousness of the situation was fully realised, a significant number of absconders were intercepted as they made their way down the Stuart Highway, but many more were well past the tentative rendezvous point. One man reached Melbourne after travelling for 13 days.

It is true that four days after the bombing there were still 278 RAAF men absent without leave. However, it is equally true that many men remained at their post, and even more returned from having complied with an order to leave the base. The airfield was never entirely abandoned as some reports suggest. The transport platoon, for example, was an harmonious, well-motivated, well-led group of men who, like so many other transport platoons in the Services, comprised the older, more mature men, whose promotion prospects were invariably limited. They lost four of their number in the second air-raid, yet the survivors all remained at their place of duty.

As a result of the shameful *débâcle*, the Station Commander was removed from his command. His intention had been merely to move his airmen to a safe rendezvous point just to the south of the base, lest another attack should be launched. A wiser, more experienced Commanding Officer might have assembled his command of 1,100 men and told them of his intentions, but it is easy to be wise on reflection. Griffith was also experiencing for the first time the terror of two comprehensive bombing attacks. Such an experience has a numbing effect on the rational thought processes. Naturally, when he passed on his orders to those officers he encountered by chance, they took on an urgency and meaning that was never intended. Some men took advantage of the situation, hearing what they wanted to hear, and they needed no encouragement not to remain for a third pounding on a post almost universally loathed.

The sight of the military fleeing down the Stuart Highway -- they were not all airmen -- had an understandably unnerving effect on the civilian population. In the second air attack, following on so soon after the first, they saw the inescapable probability of an imminent invasion. The Official War History commented that it was not surprising that many civilians left as fast as they could.

> The siren was the starting signal for civilians to enter the 'Adelaide River Stakes'. The exodus, though disgraceful in many ways, was in the best interest of the Armed Services.

The Armed Services themselves took an active, though unofficial, part in encouraging and persuading the residual civilians to leave. Among the first civilian vehicles to join the race was the sanitation bowser. Alan Powell described the nightsoil service as 'the most secure job in town'. Eight men were seen clinging to the top of the vehicle as it made its bumpy, uncomfortable progress towards the small town at Adelaide River. The noise of the contents slopping around inside was clearly audible to those refugees the vehicle passed-by in the roadway. It was the first vehicle to reach Adelaide River.

Panic was rife as civilians literally stopped what they were doing, and fled from their unsecured homes, shops and businesses to join the jam on the road to Adelaide River. For the military, the open, vacant properties seemed to be the answer to their crying needs. In an orgy of drunkenness and looting that lasted for weeks, those obliged to remain to protect the civilian property were those in the van of the town's sacking. Had there been a disciplined Provost Corps, the excesses of the Australian and American servicemen might have been frustrated. Not only did the Military Police not impose law and order but, in some cases, they were at the head of marauding groups in search of their share. The Official War History, in masterful understatement, recorded: 'The poor quality of the Provost Corps stationed in the area was noticeable. This unit did not operate in a praiseworthy manner'. The historic old Chinatown, the Chinese being at the head of the departing column, was systematically looted and burnt down until all that remained of the old site was a smoking ruin. Abbott wrote in dismay:

> Here is a town which was damaged by enemy action on one day. It was not attacked by any other means, yet in the days and weeks that followed, this Australian town was thoroughly and systematically stripped of its contents by other Australians.

The day after the Japanese raid, the vast majority of the civilian inhabitants had fled. It was estimated that only 500 had remained in the town, and most of these were the sailors from the bombed ships. On 21 February, the Darwin Area came under military command, under the orders of the GOC, Major General Blake. Civil law did not give way to martial law, and was exercised through the one remaining solitary civil constable. Abbott stayed on to tidy up until 2 March, when he moved the Administration to Alice Springs. The Services were left to organise themselves, and the area, against future Japanese initiatives.

Internationally, the news of the attack on Darwin had to compete with news of other contemporary disasters, notably the fall of Singapore only two days previously. At home, the banner headline of the *Melbourne Herald* proclaimed: '15 KILLED, 24 HURT IN DARWIN ATTACKS'.

Censorship is a prevailing theme in this trilogy, as indelibly imprinted as in a stick of peppermint rock. The severity and frequency of its imposition was surprising. Surprising in so far that Curtin rarely balked from the use of his powers, and surprising because the government had failed to appreciate that the imposition of national rules in an international arena does not prevent truth from finding a way through. The censorship imposed after the Darwin attacks had little to do with logic.

There is an Australian pre-occupation with winners and winning. News of defeat at national level is universally unwelcome, and therefore it could be argued that the government was merely withholding news that the public would not want to hear. Those who might find this assertion a little far-fetched, should reflect upon the reasons why there is so little record of the events contained in this book to be found conveniently in the places where they occurred.

It was essential, from the government's viewpoint, that they should minimise the damage that news of the surprise attack and total unpreparedness of Darwin to defend itself, might have upon the Party. Shortly afterwards, the Secretary of the Department of the Army remarked that 'Darwin is an important operational area but not a vital area in the same sense as Sydney, Newcastle and Port Kembla'. Herein lay the germinated seeds of the Monash Report, and a hint of an unofficial national strategy which will be developed in the Broome section: the existence of the so-called 'Brisbane Line'.

Curtin made a stirring speech, aimed at preparing the rest of Australia for further attacks. The speech, however, was not a valid reflection of the events that had arisen in Darwin. 'In this first battle on Australian soil', he said, 'it will be a source of pride to the public to know that the armed forces and the civilians comported themselves with the gallantry that is traditional in the people of our stock'. The public were shielded from the truth of what had really taken place at Darwin, and the press was only permitted to declare a small proportion of the actual casualties.

That there had been some economy with the truth became evident as stories from Darwin percolated south, and inconsistencies were apparent when compared with the reports released by the less-inhibited Americans. 'The bombing of Darwin was an end', wrote Alan Powell,

> the logical end to years of insularity and blind dependence, the foreseeable end to ten weeks of military reverses – and its immediate impact on the Australian people was small, because their government would not trust them with the truth and because, as an American observer said, 'Darwin, to most Australians, was . . . completely unknown . . . It's way to hell and gone up in the northwest corner'.

When Sir Paul Hasluck, years later, described the events in Darwin as 'a day of national shame', there were howls of unjustified protest.

* * *

All that, therefore, remained between the northern coast of Australia and the Japanese, now swarming with relative ease through the Dutch East Indies, was ABDA. On 25 February, ABDA was dissolved, on the very reasonable grounds that little was left to command. The exception was a Combined Naval Striking Force which, from 2 February, came under Rear Admiral K W F M Doorman, Royal Netherlands Navy.

Churchill's bitterness regarding the fate of the Striking Force was evident in *The Hinge of Fate:*

> There were elaborate arguments about whether as a compromise a Dutch Admiral might command the naval forces; how all was to be arranged with the Americans and British; where the Australians came in and so forth. Hardly had all this been agreed for the five Powers and three Services when the whole vast area concerned was conquered by the Japanese, and the combined fleet of the Allies was sunk in the forlorn battle of the Java Sea.

The first rounds of the Battle of Java Sea were fired at 16.16 hours on 27 February by two Japanese cruisers. Within two days, all but four American destroyers had succumbed to the Japanese attacks. Among the many losses were the distinguished HMAS *Perth*, the famed HMS *Exeter*, and the USS *Houston*, sunk in the Sunda Straits. She had simply run out of luck. One of the last orders issued by the acting Captain of *Houston* was to Lieutenant John D Lamade, to save himself and his observer by making their escape in the ship's Curtiss Seagull floatplane.

The USS *Houston* was off Lombok in the Dutch East Indies when Lamade received the order to leave the ship. He ran down to the wardroom and scanned a map of the world stuck to the bulkhead. He decided to make for 'a place called Broome'. He continued:

> I attempted to pick off the latitude and longitude of Broome as best I could and I went back and got into my Scout Observation Curtiss Seaplane. As we could see the Japanese planes approaching we could see they were going to bomb us again, they shot me off and I took a south-easterly course toward Broome.

BROOME

3. Broome

In 1883, Broome was named after Sir Frederick Napier Broome, the newly-arrived Governor of the Colony of Western Australia with its capital in Perth. The Governor's sense of pride, pleasure and feeling of honour was soon to be diminished when his subsequent investigations revealed that the town consisted of little more than temporary, insanitary, mosquito-infested pearling camps. Feeling decidedly underwhelmed, he attempted unsuccessfully to dissociate himself from the dubious honour.

Broome does, of course, predate the official gazetting of its founding on 21 November 1883. The town is located on the Dampier Peninsula, so-named after the celebrated explorer who visited the region in 1688 aboard the privateer *Cygnet*. The truth about Dampier is that his reputation was earned not through a somewhat indifferent career at sea but rather by the contents of his celebrated journals. These provided an illuminating, illustrated record of his voyages to northern Australia, the Indies and many other countries. On his return to England he wrote, *A New Voyage Around the World*. The book was an instant success. So inspired was the famous English satirist, Jonathan Swift, that he based his book, *Gulliver's Travels*, on Dampier's exploits, locating, so we are led to believe, Lilliput somewhere to the north of Broome.

The appetites of Their Lordships of the Admiralty had been whetted by the descriptions of Dampier's journeys. They gave him a commission in the Royal Navy and an old, barely-seaworthy vessel, HMS *Roebuck*, and in 1699, encouraged him to return once again to Australia. It had been Dampier's intention to sail to the south of the continent but the poor state of his ship, combined with the prevailing wild winter sea conditions, prevented him from taking that course of action. Instead, with great reluctance, the explorer was obliged to retrace the journey he had made aboard *Cygnet* along Australia's northern coastline. Short of food and water, he anchored in the vicinity of what Lieutenant Philip Parker King RN would, in 1821, name as Roebuck Bay. Boats were put ashore and wells dug in the fruitless search for water. The Aborigines who came down to see what the white men were doing impressed Dampier not in the slightest. He had, however, toyed with the notion of capturing a native to display to the English public. When the human souvenir was grabbed, he showed great reluctance to acquiesce with Dampier's plans. All hell was let loose. Dampier's men were obliged to abandon their quest for water, retreating hurriedly before an agitated group of Aborigines. Dampier is recorded in history as the first white man to kill an Aborigine, shot in the mêlée. Dampier and his crew sailed northward towards Timor to resume the search for water, never again to visit Australia.

Dampier's voyages around northern Australia were certainly preceded by Dutch and Portuguese explorers, but they had not been quite so meticulous in their record-keeping. In the library aboard the renowned HMS *Beagle* was a copy of Dampier's book. It was this which, in all probability, had prompted Lieutenant Stokes to drop anchor on 15 January 1838 in Roebuck Bay, prior to his discovery of Port Darwin. He, too, did not enjoy a memorable experience ashore in this unremarkable and uncompromising land. The negligent discharge of a musket severely wounded the Chief Surveyor. Aroused by the sound of the weapon, a group of Aborigines appeared, threatening to attack. The sailors' mission was to reconnoitre rather than fight so, picking up the wounded officer, they terminated their survey and sailed away in the *Beagle*.

Gradually, Broome developed. The pearlers lived in reasonable harmony with the Aborigines, whose services as divers they shamefully exploited. Nevertheless, despite a harsh disciplinary regime and rigid segregation, there was rarely any conflict between the natives and maritime industries over the subject of land rights. The pearlers had their eyes turned exclusively towards the sea; it was the pastoralists who, from the mid-1860s, struggled with the Aborigines for land ownership. Eventually, the harshness of the climate and the dawning realisation that the environs of Broome were not best suited to agricultural endeavour, eased the prospect of continuing bloody conflict between native and settler. By the turn of the century, the population of Broome could focus its attention almost entirely on the harvest of shell and pearl from the sea.

Until the 1880s, skin-diving had been the sole means of retrieving pearl shell but, as the convenient supply was exhausted, the unprotected divers were drawn towards the dangers of the deeper water. The problems of how to reach the rich, deep beds was overcome by the introduction of the diving-suit with its traditional weighted boots and round diving-helmet. Unfortunately for the Aborigine, the new technology was to prove to be completely beyond his mastery. Almost overnight, he was to disappear as a diving force.

The introduction of the new diving technique in the pearling industry coincided with the development of a political goal to be promulgated in 1902 and known as The White Australia Policy. The Japanese had been quick to demonstrate their superiority over other nationals, both in operating the new gear and in the amount of shell that they were able to gather. They were natives of Wakayama, tucked away in the south-east corner of Honshu. The people from this region have by tradition followed Nakimini-Fudo, the God of the Sea, and are by reputation highly capable divers and fishermen.

Half-hearted attempts to replace the Japanese by former Royal Navy divers had quite disastrous repercussions for the latter. The experiment had not been a success, and the message the pearlers had returned to the politicians was, 'We told you so'. The income from pearling prior to the Great War was important to the economy; sufficiently important for a compromise to be reached. Working Asian divers were, therefore, permitted to remain in Broome but, as the new policy took effect, the divers' dependants were not admitted as immigrants. From this point on, Japanese domination of the diving scene in the distinctive helmeted suit was never satisfactorily contested. They maintained their pre-eminent position right up to 1941 when over 500 of them were providing Broome with the wherewithal to develop its wealth and livelihood.

The bubble was burst by Pearl Harbor and Australia's prompt declaration of war on Japan. Broome's outnumbered Europeans were obliged to initiate a contingency plan more thorough than Darwin's which provided for the internment of all Japanese. That these Japanese had spent all or a significant part of their lives in Australia, were now married and had children who had been born in Australia, was no justification for exemption from the plan for imprisonment of all Japanese. The trawl was so thorough that it included Jimmy Chi born in Broome of a Chinese father and Japanese mother. 'The white people here reckoned I was communicating with the Japanese and my brother was in the Japanese air force.' The divers were philosophical and began to fill Broome's inadequate prison, where the régime was relaxed, friendly and apologetic. As luggers returned to port after their two-three month stint at sea, the Japanese crews pulled them up onto the beach and were then escorted to gaol. The Japanese made no attempt to seize the luggers and sail them back to Honshu.

The European townspeople were naturally distressed to see their respected workers and breadwinners treated in such a manner, but they were powerless to intervene. They did much to ease the discomfiture of the Japanese by bringing presents and gifts of food to the prisoners in the crowded gaol. The divers were given a warm farewell when the time came for them to walk along the wooden jetty to board the ship which would take them on the first leg of their long journey to internment camps in the south.

* * *

Today, the town of Broome, Western Australia, and its surrounding shire has a population of 6,000 and covers an area of 56,000 square kilometres; three times the size of Wales. The State capital, Perth, lies 2,213 kilometres to the south. The Indonesian island of Timor lies 900 kilometres to the north. In very general terms, the climate is similar to that of Darwin in so far as there is a dry and a wet season and the area is susceptible to the visits of cyclones.

The economy of the town is no longer dependent upon the search for pearl shell. A flourishing cultured-pearl industry has been developed, and oil and agriculture also make a contribution. The major industry today, however, is tourism, which promises to grow at an even faster rate now that a sealed road goes right around Australia. The pursuit of the tourist's dollar is reflected in the rebuilding of the famed Continental Hotel and the development of the 1883 Roebuck Bay Hotel. The latter establishment has struck a sensible compromise between the new and the old. Provision has been made for the gastronomic expectations of the well-to-do tourists in a couth corner of the pub, yet the atmosphere of the historic old bar, opening out into Dampier Terrace, has thankfully been preserved. On the other side of the Terrace are the old pearling sheds backing onto a mangrove-fringed estuary. Streeters Jetty, built in 1879, still remains as a witness to the decline of the industry from its heyday, when 400 luggers worked the pearlfields. Today, the number is down to four or five.

The residents of Broome will tell you that theirs is the most cosmopolitan town in Australia. A visit to the old Chinatown reveals street signs in English, Japanese, Chinese, Malay and Arabic. It is not as congested as it was, but the buildings here date from the 1900s. The character of the area is preserved and protected by local ordinance. It was the former presence of this cocktail of Asians which prompted the initiation in 1970 of a rather special festival. Shinju

Matsuri, or Festival of Pearl, has developed into one of Australia's most popular and best-known cultural festivals. With extraordinary foresight, the organising committee in ten days of celebration, is able to include, among others, the Chinese Festival of Hung Ting, the Japanese Bon Festival and the Malaysian Merdeka. This annual event, held during August-September, attracts 20,000-30,000 tourists to the town.

The old Court House provides an inkling of a further aspect of Broome's development. In 1888, the Eastern Extension Australasian and China Telegraph Company decided to link Broome with Banjoewangi in the Dutch East Indies by a submarine cable. The Court House was the original cable house containing transmitting equipment until it became redundant in 1914. The nearby beach, however, one of Australia's most beautiful unspoilt beaches, has retained the name, Cable Beach.

There is not a great deal by way of physical evidence that remains of the Japanese who, with smaller numbers of Koepangers, Filipinos, Chinese and Malays, made Broome a pre-war little Asia in Australia. In the town is a low, white-painted and shuttered building with a diver's helmet mounted above the entrance – the Japanese Divers' Club. It is outside the town, however, that significant evidence of the former existence of those wiry folk from Wakayama can be found – in the Japanese Cemetery.

The Japanese Cemetery at Broome has none of the symmetry of the Japanese War Cemetery at Cowra. The older headstones dating from 1896, made of sandstone and beach rock, contrast with replacement tombstones fashioned from black granite. The refurbishment of those stones which had not stood the passage of time dates from 1983 and was made possible through the generous donation of $160,000 by a Japanese philanthropist, Mr Ryoichi Sasakama. That the dead are of the Shinto faith is evident from the bottles embedded in the tombstones. Each year, on 15 August, the Japanese honour their dead at the festival of Obom by making offerings of saki, food and flowers to the spirits of the departed.

These are not the graves of old men. When the Japanese diver had worked his fill, he withdrew his money from the bank, returning to his homeland and retirement. On one small headstone, a memorial to five men, their ages are given as 21 (2), 26, 28 and 29. In the graveyard there are 707 graves representing 919 men. A tall obelisk rising from the middle of the cemetery commemorates those who drowned in a cyclone on 26 April 1908. 'In that year, near La Grange Mission,

41 luggers were sunk and 40 men died. This memorial was built by the survivors.' In addition, the memorial records that in 1887, and again in 1935, 140 men were killed on each occasion by cyclones. The weather was not the sole killer. The bends, or diver's paralysis, accounted for many of those in the graveyard. In the year 1914, 33 men lost their lives in that manner. No better testament can exist to the awful dangers inherent in the pearling trade and the utter willingness of the Japanese to take their lives to the very threshold of death and beyond. They were a proud people for whom pecuniary reward was an obvious factor, but it also had a lot to do with that peculiarly Asiatic trait known as 'face'.

Notwithstanding the growth and development of the town, it still retains a frontier spirit, due in part to its remoteness from the centres of high density population. As an illustration, the author was surprised when, on his last visit to Broome in 1986, he found in his room in the prestigious Continental Hotel a notice, earnestly requesting guests to wear footwear in the dining room. There are those who take advantage of Broome's relative isolation, which is reflected in a plethora of enforcement agencies – Federal Police, State Police, Customs Service, Coast Watch – some with overlapping and duplicated responsibilities. The evidence of smuggling is seen in the town's singular blemish, that of drug abuse. As one agent admitted, 'our priority is to catch the supplier, not the user'. The organised criminal has a wide selection of isolated landing areas in which to put down light aircraft coming in undetected from the north. The risks are low, the profits high.

The Continental Hotel lies to the east of the town on the site of the original hotel overlooking Roebuck Bay. From the foreshore it is possible, a few times in the year, to witness a phenomenon known as the Golden Staircase to the Moon. This is caused by the light of the rising moon reflecting from the ocean bed during the low water spring tide. To the west of the hotel is a reserve known as Bedford Park which contains the war memorial and other artefacts from Broome's past. One item on display here is relevant to the development of this story. It is as though it were a piece of a jigsaw puzzle which, when amalgamated with the other pieces to be found, in the aviation display in a grounded DC3, in the library, and among the relics on show at the Broome Historical Museum, add up to a complete picture of the events which happened here on 3 March 1942. An expert would be able to tell the reader that the item under examination is a Dornier motor from a Do.24 Flying Boat of the type flown by the Royal

Netherlands Naval Air Arm during the War. Closer examination reveals bullet holes in the engine nacelle and on the propeller blades. The engine was recovered from the nearby Roebuck Bay. The reason for it being there and its condition had nothing to do with rising moons but rather with Rising Suns.

*   *   *

The news of the bombing of Darwin sent a shock-wave through the nation. On 20 February 1942, southern cities experienced their first practice air-raid alert. Legislation was initiated for the mandatory provision of air-raid shelters at the workplace. Meanwhile, the remoteness and complete sense of isolation of the front-line towns of Port Hedland, Derby and Wyndham was being acutely felt. They were sitting targets should the Japanese feel the inclination to attack. Broome, in particular, was tempting providence through the increased number of flights into Java of arms and armaments to support the last-ditch stand of the Dutch. As munitions and equipment went in, non-effectives, wounded and refugees came out. Eventually, no further shipments were consigned to Tjilatjap, the point of entry into Java, the emphasis being placed now on the evacuation of servicemen and dependants as the Japanese tightened the ring from three sides. In two weeks in February, an estimated 8,000 servicemen and refugees had been evacuated through Broome.

The aircraft called forward to cope with the airlift were many and various, from the air forces of Australia, Britain, the Netherlands and the United States, as well as those of Australian and Dutch civil carriers. Using Broome as a base, the planes gathered like bees around a honey pot. On one day alone, 57 aircraft arrived in the town. With Darwin bombed, the convenience of Broome, with its limited but sheltered Bay for flying-boat operations and a long, all-weather sealed airstrip, was fully exploited. How soon it would be before Japan took remedial action against the Allied activity, was open to conjecture. That the operation was so overt, that there was no provision of anti-aircraft guns in the town and no fighter cover, was due to a strange strategic misappreciation that Broome was beyond the range of Japanese aircraft. It was convenient to believe that Broome's security was derived from its distance from the seat of war.

The decision to evacuate compulsorily the women and children of Broome was taken on 23 February. Places were made available aboard ships of the State Shipping Service, which called in to collect their passengers from the jetty. Only one white woman remained in town, Mrs Marjorie Bardwell, the determined telephonist, who operated the post office's exchange. For the men who had not followed the flag to war, there was little option but to remain *in situ*. The roads leading out of town had been closed by the seasonal wet weather. Their services were channelled towards the local war effort. At the beginning of March, though a considerable hive of activity, Broome was in effect a toothless tiger. There was no offensive air support, no naval ships, and the only army representation was to be found in the elderly soldiers of the Volunteer Defence Corps (VDC). The VDC's equipment establishment included six .303 rifles and an entitlement to 30 boxes of ball ammunition.

By 2 March, the airlift had passed its peak. By now the aircrews had worked themselves into a state of exhaustion. Out in Roebuck Bay, at mid-day, sat three flying-boats with empty fuel tanks. A tender, the 56-ton *Nicol Bay*, moved slowly among them, unable to cope with the vagaries of the ten-metre tide, her rudimentary hand-pump equipment, or the thirst of the aircraft. At least a further dozen flying-boats were working out of the Bay but were currently on operations, to return to Broome by last light, with tired crews and empty fuel tanks.

Out at the airfield, every parking bay was usually full. The state of the soggy ground, softened by continual rain, forced the local commander to park the mix of Liberators, Lodestars, Flying Fortresses and Hudsons wing-to-wing on the limited amount of available hardstanding. Everywhere, in the airport buildings, hotels and boarding-rooms would be the countless sleeping bodies of passengers in transit and aircrew, who had slipped into the complacent frame of mind that, having reached this north-west corner of Australia, the worst was now behind them.

At 3 pm, when the majority of Broome's temporarily-resident transport aircraft were in the air answering to diverse tasks, there appeared in the overcast sky above the town a Japanese Betty reconnaissance aircraft. The plane maintained a height of 4,000 metres and, without interruption, leisurely circled the town, the crew photographing and making notes before heading northward in the direction from whence it had come.

The Qantas seaplane operations out of Broome had grown even before the bombing of Darwin, when the Sydney–Singapore transit facility was transferred there from Darwin as a precautionary measure. The company's Short Empire Class flying-boats, still operating in company livery, were among the very first to start the evacuation of refugees from the Dutch East Indies. They were, too, among the first to suffer casualties when the *Corio,* on a mission evacuating women and children from Sourabaya, was shot down on 30 January near Koepang. Thirteen crew members and passengers were lost. The staff of Qantas Empire Airways, therefore, had good reason for caution. Their slow, lumbering craft were entirely unsuited to be operating as front-line aircraft. They were the shire horse breed of the family, better suited to operations in rear areas, behind screens of agile fighters and a comprehensive air-defence system.

The Captain in charge of Qantas air operations in Broome, Captain L J Brain, watched the *Betty* fly off to the north. The *Corinthian* had only just touched down from the northern islands, but one of her sister ships, the *Circe,* which had taken off at the same time, was now overdue, never to be seen or heard of again. The Captain, therefore, had good reason to believe that Broome was living on borrowed time.

The State Shipping Service's coastal steamer *Koolama* was bombed and disabled by the Japanese off Cape Londonderry. One of the planes in the Qantas fleet, the *Camilla,* was diverted that afternoon to pick up the 25 survivors who were now ashore. The *Camilla* was no stranger to the war. She had been anchored in Darwin harbour just off the jetty, near to *Neptuna* and *Barossa,* when the port was bombed. Amazingly, she was unscathed, due in part to being hidden from the view of the bomber pilots by the profusion of black smoke arising from the two ships. When her crew examined her fragile shell, they were astounded to find that among all the surrounding devastation, she remained airworthy. She took off through the smoke and débris to assume an easterly course. Three minutes after she had taken to the air, *Neptuna* exploded.

Not wishing to have all his eggs in one basket, Brain ordered *Camilla*'s skipper to stay clear of Broome until after 11 am on 3 March. His remarkable foresight was to save craft, crew and passengers. *Camilla* continued in service for over another year, finally being destroyed on 22 April 1943 in a landing accident off Port Moresby.

During the night of 2 March, a Japanese flying-boat was tasked to make a final, confirmatory reconnaissance over Broome. At 2 am the next morning, the navigator was able to pick out a pre-arranged signal from the end of the jetty, given, presumably, by a fifth columnist. As an unexpected bonus, the airfield turned on the tower lights in the mistaken belief that the Japanese plane was an overdue Liberator bomber. Much the same kind of security lapse was to occur again at Mascot airport in Sydney, where the authorities were able to help orientate a Japanese reconnaissance plane supporting a submarine attack, by turning on the runway lights.

Nine hundred kilometres to the north at 335 Air Base in Koepang, a flight of ten aircraft from the Japanese Third Naval Air Group took off at 07.05, destination Broome. In the hotels and boarding houses, the majority of the aircrews were enjoying a leisurely awakening, with the prospect of breakfast followed by a visit to the bar. The 'she'll be right' syndrome was again to leave its mark on affairs Australian.

Out at the airfield, the Liberator which had been expected that night had made its belated appearance and was in the process of being refuelled. The pilot and co-pilot, Lieutenants Kester and Ragdale, were occupied in the USAAF Operations Room checking their flight plan for the next stage of the aero-medical evacuation of their passengers, US servicemen wounded in Java.

Compared with the massive pre-emptive attack on Darwin, the impending raid on Broome was small beer, probably intended to achieve nothing more than to maintain pressure on Australia, emphasising her sense of isolation. In these early months, it was part of Japan's expressed strategic thinking to cut Australia off from her allies in order that, according to Tokyo radio: 'With her limited manpower and war industries, should she continue to wage war on Japan, she will inevitably collapse'. A further attack on Darwin was approved for 4 March but, for the moment, the nine Zero fighters and one Babs reconnaissance aircraft were well into their scheduled two and a half hour flight to Broome. A further eight Zeros were concurrently en route to Wyndham on a similar mission.

The Broome raid was led by Lieutenant Zenziro Miyamo. In his briefing, he had been ordered to select military targets only. His initial plan was to divide his Mitsubishi A6M2 Zero aircraft into three groups of three. One group was assigned to the airfield, one to the harbour, and the third, as a reserve, would provide air-cover. It is not entirely clear what the pilots expected to achieve. Japanese Intelligence would have been aware that the air-lift was in its last throes. The daylight reconnaissance of the previous day had shown only three flying-boats at their moorings. Consequently, the Zeros were not carrying full ammunition loads in the interest of extending their range. What an unexpected bonanza was awaiting the arrival of the Japanese aircraft. Below each plane hung belly-drop tanks with an additional capacity of 320 litres of fuel. The Zeros, therefore, had a range of approximately 2,000 kilometres, allowing sufficient reserve to permit some time over the target.

The morning of Tuesday, 3 March had broken warm and sunny over Broome. The incoming tide lapped against the hulls of the flying-boats, some of which were moored up to 1,500 metres from the shore. The craft responded by moving, imperceptibly at first, until the water underneath lifted them from the muddy bottom. On board many of the most distant planes were Dutch refugees, women and children. Problems in ferrying them ashore, plus a shortage of accommodation, meant that they had had to endure a hot, uncomfortable night aboard the aircraft. During the night, the *Nicol Bay* had plied between the sleeping giants. Dogged by difficulties, including aircrew apathy, she was only able to refuel three craft.

Out on the terrace of the Continental Hotel, the by-now breakfasted aircrews were engaged in conversation, bidding farewell while enjoying the first beer of the day. It was 9.20 am. Barely in the air above Broome was the aero-medical evacuation Liberator. Out on Roebuck Bay, Lamade had completed his flight checks and was readying for take-off. The sound of unfamiliar aircraft above the Bay, and the sight of the unmistakable red roundels on the silver aircraft, confirmed to those who had assembled at the Continental that they had dallied too long. The Japanese had arrived.

* * *

Sitting in the hotel writing a letter to the Managing Director was Qantas' Captain Lester Brain. He was still weak from a bout of dengue fever which causes loss of appetite and dependence on fluids. In his case, he had spent the previous week on milk and soda water. Brain's diary of 3 March recalls:

> Am interrupted by the unmistakable sound of machine guns and pop outside the hotel to see a number of Japanese fighters diving on and shooting up the flying-boats in the harbour. Got over to the shore and stood by watching it. There are 15 boats and three of them are already alight and burning furiously.

Stung into action by the shouts and screams from the Bay, Brain rushed to the shore to get a dinghy into the water. The fever had drained him and he could not budge the small craft. He was helped by a man named Malcolm Millar and together they took their small boat towards the flames on a brave rescue mission. They pulled out of the water a mother and her child, a boy and three of the most distressed of the many men found in the water. Desperately overloaded, they took the small rowing boat back to the nearest mangrove beach. 'Meanwhile to my surprise', continued Brain,

> I noticed that although all the flying-boats were destroyed, two luggers which had been engaged on refuelling (one was the *Nicol Bay*) were apparently undamaged and were rescuing other survivors in apparently large numbers.

The thoughts and reflections of those who had witnessed the attack on Broome were to become a matter of interest to the Marine Staff at the Dutch Ministry of Defence. The Director of Naval History later recorded:

> So far as is known, only a few of the survivors of the Broome raid are still alive today, among them perhaps one or two of the pilots who were involved in the evacuation from the Dutch East Indies. About ten years ago (1978) the Department of History tried to interview some of the surviving crew members about the circumstances in which the rescue took place. The result was negative. Practically all of them declined to give us the information requested. Apparently they did not like to be reminded because of a still vivid personal grief about relatives lost on that 'black Tuesday' when the Japanese fighter pilots caught the Dutch crews completely by surprise.

There is little doubt that the pilots would have been tired but one local historian said that many had been drinking heavily. Attempts were made to ascertain why the flying-boats' pilots had not heeded the warnings to clear Broome at the first opportunity. Captain Harold Mathiesen, the heroic skipper of the *Nicol Bay*, gave evidence before the RAAF Board.

> I can not understand why the boats which had refuelled did not take off early that morning. Even at 8 am, when I was alongside the jetty, there was ample water available to transport people out to the boats [flying-boats]. The float plane belonging to the USS *Houston* was right on the beach and she got away a quarter of an hour before the raid, the other flying-boats had plenty of water.

Having awaited the return of the tide, the *Nicol Bay* had been engaged in the refuelling of the Short *Corinna* when the Zeros struck. Fortunately for the 25 passengers, they were still waiting for the boats to take them out to the plane. They threw themselves down as the fighters, now unencumbered by belly-tanks, swooped on the flying-boats in their sights. The earlier Japanese plan was aborted as all the Zero fighters sought out pickings from the surprising array of targets below them. The dutiful Babs kept a watchful eye above the massacre unfolding below.

Machine-gun and cannon-fire tore into *Corinna* as the crew abandoned ship, diving deep into the water, the surface of which was ablaze with aviation fuel. Systematically, the Japanese took full advantage of their good fortune by the leisurely and unopposed destruction of each flying-boat in the Bay. Screaming, battered and bloodied refugees struggled to escape the fire raging through the planes by tumbling into the conflagration of a fiery sea. Those who struggled out of the aircraft nearest the shore 'became mired, some waist deep in the mud and muck, struggling to get to solid ground. Some were killed and wounded in the aircraft and in the attempt to get to the shore', said American pilot Richard A Legg. Another American pilot, Frank Kurtz, also witnessed the attack.

> I saw one Dutchman swim ashore dragging his wife by the hair. The whole lower half of her face had been blown away and she was dead. I saw another woman standing on the wing of one of the planes which was burning. She had a child in her arms, and was ready to jump and swim ashore, when a cannon shot hit her in the back and broke her into halves. They both fell forward into the water, but the arms on the top half which held the child never let go of it.

The captain of a visiting refuelling ship gave Lamade, the pilot of the *Houston*'s seaplane, orders to head for Perth. Arrangements were made for them to make rendezvous at Exmouth Gulf on 3 March. Lamade was up early that morning. The tide was still out but turning, and the little aircraft was still high and dry. It was, therefore, relatively easy for him to help his radio man by the name of Tubbs into the rear seat. The man was suffering from dengue fever and thus unable to operate either the radio or .30 machine gun. 'I got the anchor up, put it in the forward part of the main float and got all set to take off as soon as my plane floated.' In common with all the other pilots in Broome that morning, Lamade had been advised to be clear of the town by 10 am, considered to be the earliest time by which the Japanese could launch an air attack. The time estimate would prove over-optimistic, but Lamade's long-running experiences with the Japanese while aboard USS *Houston*, encouraged him to allow a margin for error. Around him, like whales stranded on the mud, was an unique collection of 16 flying-boats, Shorts, Dorniers and Catalinas.

Lamade noticed at the end of the long pier three pilots of the flying-boats lying out in the deep water. They obviously did not need to wait for the tide but were waiting instead for a boat to take them to their aircraft already overfull with passengers for the onward journey south. One American pilot recollects the women and children being 'stacked in like cordwood'. As soon as his 100 miles an hour seaplane was afloat, Lamade took off 'and flew right over the end of the dock and I sort of waved goodbye to the pilots and just then, I think it was, about six Japanese Zero fighter planes came zooming down'.

The veteran ace pilot, Warrant-Officer Osama Kudo, spotted the movement of Lamade's floatplane below him. It was the only aircraft making any positive attempt to escape. He fired a burst at the navy plane, missed, and then flew his Zero into a better position to make absolutely certain of destroying the slow, helpless floatplane. As the Japanese banked, his attention was caught by the momentary sight of a Liberator escaping over the sea to the north. He aborted his attack on the less-attractive floatplane in favour of the higher-value target, which happened to be Lieutenant Kester's aero-medical flight.

Kester's loss was Lamade's gain, for the young navy pilot's was the only allied aircraft to escape from Broome that day. Soon, the Liberator was overhauled and sent seaward in flames, ten kilometres off Cable Beach. It stayed afloat long enough for two Marine Sergeants to escape, the only two to survive out of an aircraft complement of 33. USAAF requests to Lester Brain to mount an air search-and-rescue mission were turned down, giving rise to unnecessary ill-feeling. All Brain had available was the *Camilla*, already tasked on a vital job. The American Commander, Colonel Legg was reluctant to use his Broome-based bombers and as a compromise, the Qantas staff took out a 30ft launch to search the crash area.

While the two Sergeants set out upon the long swim south,* Kudo was above the airfield. The attacks in the Bay had taken only 15 minutes. While small craft plied between the burning wreckage in search of survivors, the Japanese had moved off in search of additional targets. Over on the airfield, where a mix of six bombers and transports were still on the ground, pilots and crews were conscientiously putting time to good effect prior to their prearranged sorties out of Broome during the course of the day. The noise coming from

---

* Both reached the shore after 32 hours in the water but one, severely weakened by the ordeal, died on his way to hospital. The survivor, a Sergeant M O Donoho was found naked walking up the runway. He was in reasonable condition after a day fighting the tide and suffering the anguish of swimming in shark-infested water. On four occasions the tide took him back out to sea when almost ashore. He was casevacked to Melbourne on 5 March.

Roebuck Bay provided the essential warning for those on the airfield to dive for cover. In the event, there were to be no casualties here during this raid.

The Zeros made low, strafing passes and, very soon, all the grounded aircraft were ablaze. Incensed, a Dutchman loaded a .303 machine-gun and, firing from the shoulder engaged the Japanese aircraft pre-occupied in their orgy of destruction. Kudo's Zero shuddered. Leaving behind a trail of black smoke, it headed seaward where it crashed, killing the pilot.

The Dutch officer was 6 foot 4 inch 2nd Lieutenant W F A Winckel. He suffered severe burns to his left hand but this did not prevent him from flying two further refugee missions to Bandung. For his bravery he was awarded the Netherlands Bronze Cross – equivalent to the Distinguished Service Order. His heroism did not end here for on 4 June 1942, while assigned to Number 10 (NL) Squadron at Canberra and flying a B-25 Mitchell bomber, he sank a Japanese submarine off the coast of Newcastle.*

Gus Winckel's personal account of the raid on Broome is illuminating:

> I had just landed in Broome at approximately 8 am on 3 March 1942 after a seven hour flight from Bandung in Java. I taxied to the refuelling place and cut the engines. The passengers had left the aircraft and I picked up my flight plan and flight bag and also descended from the rear door. Whilst I stretched myself, I saw some specks on the northern horizon and asked the refuelling attendant if they had some RAAF aircraft flying around. He shook his head, so I told him to sound the alarm as Japanese aircraft were approaching. His answer with a smile was 'That is impossible, they do not come this far south'.
>
> There was no airfield defence at all. The Japanese could have landed and taken Broome without a shot being fired. We were so ill-prepared. My aircraft was a Lockheed Lodestar which had two .303 Colt removable air-cooled machine-guns in mountings at the rear window on either side of the aircraft. As luck would have it, the Zeros attacked the Catalinas in the Bay first, which game me time to herd the passengers into a kind of shelter, big cement pipe culverts, also to enter the Lodestar again to remove a machine gun and its fixed ammo box (400 rounds) from its mounting. Something told me what was in store and I searched for a suitable place to attack the strafing Zeros. I was well prepared and waited for my chance. It was not long before they came in low from the Bay to attack the sitting ducks. A B24 (Liberator) took

---

* 35°22' South/152°36' East. Winckel dropped a stick of six 300lb bombs on the submarine. 'It could not have been better', he said. 'The path of the bombs followed the length of the vessel, and it seemed to us above that every one of them hit it somewhere.'

off and was only just airborne when it was shot down and sadly crashed and burnt. Of the crew and eight passengers,* only one survived to tell the tale. It made my blood boil.

One Zero came in low to strafe my Lodestar and it came for me in the most favourable direction. Holding the barrel of the gun with my left hand and the handles against my shoulder, I gave it a long burst of fire. After it passed me (plus or minus ten yards) I saw a trail of smoke coming from the aircraft and she disappeared towards the Bay. Later I was told it crashed there. My Lodestar did not burn but it was a total write-off. Luckily my second Lodestar had some engine trouble prior to take-off from Bandung and it was delayed for half an hour. The pilot, Sergeant-Major Kranenburg, saw the black smoke from Broome on the horizon and turned away. He landed half an hour later. He could not stay in the air any longer because his petrol tanks were almost empty.

With this aircraft we flew the wounded and passengers to Port Hedland and Perth and even had to carry the evacuees in the nose luggage compartment as ballast, as, of course, all their possessions were burned or got lost. (There are no windows in the nose of the aircraft, only darkness.) It took us two days to clear the backlog of wounded and evacuees.

I was never awarded a medal (Australian) for this; all I got out of this adventure was a badly burned left hand. I noticed and felt the pain after the air-raid was over. Nevertheless, I still had to continue flying the wounded and the evacuees.

By 10.30 am the Japanese aircraft were on their way back to base, well satisfied with their performance, and jubilant at their good fortune in finding such a proliferation of aircraft. They had stayed over their target longer than planned and had used over half their fuel. One Zero was to crash off an island 100 kilometres south of Koepang, but the pilot rejoined his unit 18 days later. All but one of the surviving Zeros suffered bullet damage, and one pilot had been slightly wounded. It conjures in the imagination what might have been achieved had Broome airfield been provided with a modicum of air-defence equipment manned by motivated and determined defenders.

In the air at 10.30 am, as the Japanese headed north, was the *Camilla*, resuming her journey to Broome, while approaching from the north was a camouflaged Douglas DC3 of KNILM, the Royal Dutch East Indies Airline. At sea, the re-crewed American freighter *Admiral Halstead*, fortunate to have survived her ordeal at Darwin, and still laden with aviation fuel, was nearing the jetty at Broome. Any one of these impending arrivals could have coincided with the return

---

* The account of the numbers on board varies. It seems that there were over 30 on the aircraft.

1.
The last moments
of HMS *Exeter* in
the Battle of the
Java Sea 1 March
1942 *(Taken from a
Japanese aircraft.
Source unknown)*

2. USS *Houston*. Like Exeter, she too would be sunk on 1 March 1942 and in the same great battle. *(Source unknown)*

3. 19 February 1942. A Japanese pilot's view of Darwin *(AWM) (100806)*

4. *Neptuna* and *Barossa* ablaze and shrouded in smoke alongside the jetty: Darwin *(AWM) (128107)*

5. Darwin: all that was left of two of the Wirraways that never got off the ground *(AWM) (26980)*

6. The day after. The wreck of *Neptuna* lying alongside the badly damaged wharf: Darwin *(AWM) (27329)*

7. The bombing of Darwin Post Office *(AWM) (12307)*

8. Adelaide River NT: the last resting place of those who died in the attack on the Post Office *(ARGC)*

9. Broome: the jetty *(AWM)* *(51751)*

10. Broome: 2 March 1942. All that was left of a Flying Fortress caught on the ground *(AWM)* *(42694)*

11a. Dutch Maritime Patrol Aircraft. Catalina *(Royal Netherlands Air Force Museum)*

11b. Dutch Maritime Patrol Aircraft. Do.24 *(Royal Netherlands Air Force Museum)*

12. The Mangrove Estuary, Broome and an abandoned Pearling Lugger *(ARGC)*

13. Broome: the Japanese Cemetery *(ARGC)*

14. The 12th Australian Prisoner-of-War Camp, Cowra. B Compound (*AWM*) (*67175*)

15. Cowra: after the breakout. Blankets on the wire *(AWM) (73484)*

16. The morning after: all that was left of B Compound on Saturday 5 August 1944 (*AWM*) (*73485*)

17. Assorted weapons gathered up after the breakout: Cowra *(AWM) (73486)*

18.
The price of honour. The body of Sergeant Major Masao Kojuna, Kanazawa's deputy *(AWM) (44170)*

19. Having escaped, this prisoner committed suicide. The knife with which he cut his own throat is still held firmly in his right hand *(AWM) (44171)*

20. Where Lieutenant Harry Doncaster was murdered *(ARGC)*

21. Cowra: all that remains of the camp – the entrance *(ARGC)*

22. Cairn marking the point of breakout from B Compound *(ARGC)*

23. Cowra: Ishidoro in the Japanese
War Cemetery *(ARGC)*

24. The Commonwealth Section in the Cowra War Cemetery. In the background lie
the graves of the Australians killed at Cowra *(ARGC)*

25. The 1944 Battlefield today (*ARGC*)

of the Japanese, and none possessed any suitable defence. Such is the fortune of war, and the role the element of luck plays for some – but not for others.

Camilla touched down safely at 11.15 am in Roebuck Bay amidst a scene of complete destruction and desolation. Her sister ships, *Corinna* and *Centaurus*, the latter on charter to the RAAF, were smouldering wrecks. So, too, were five Dorniers and four Catalinas of the Royal Netherlands Naval Air Arm, two United States Navy Catalinas, and two Royal Air Force Catalinas. *Corinna* was the only non-military target to have been hit. Even the vulnerable, volatile *Nicol Bay* had been spared by the Japanese pilots.

Not so fortunate had been the KNILM DC3. Her journey to Broome had started from Bandung airfield at 1 am that morning. Immediately before take-off from the beleaguered town, a small, well-wrapped and sealed box was thrust at the former White Russian air ace, but now naturalised Dutch pilot, Captain Ivan Smirnov, impatiently awaiting clearance for take-off. When the indignant pilot asked what the cigar-box-sized package contained, he was told not to worry about it. It was to be collected from him when he touched down at Broome. Eventually, after an interminable delay, Smirnov was cleared to go.

Inside the cargo plane were seven passengers; five Dutch pilots and a mother with her baby. The woman sat in the only seat in the aircraft hold. Throughout the night, the aircraft clawed itself slowly but remorselessly through the sky. At 10 am, the Australian coast came into view. As the aircraft drew nearer, the smoke from the fires of Broome could be seen. The pilot was perplexed, but the appearance of three Zeros concentrated his mind on the survival of his aircraft, crew and passengers. They had the misfortune to bump into a returning flight from Broome led by Lieutenant Zenziro Miyano.

In the first pass, Smirnov the pilot, mother and child, and another passenger, were hit as the DC3 sought in desperation to evade the attention of the nimble Zeros. Soon, the port engine burst into flames and the plane went down. With great skill, the injured pilot landed his stricken aircraft on the beach at Carnot Bay, 80 kilometres north of Broome. The Japanese persisted and, in a subsequent attack, the mechanic was shot through both knees.

For four days, the party remained on the beach, short of food and water. Four of the wounded died, including the mother and her baby. Hopes were to be raised by the appearance of a flying-boat, but it proved to be Japanese and attacked the survivors with bombs. On 6

March, a pair of RAAF Wirraways dropped food and water, with a message to the effect that help from the Beagle Bay Mission was close at hand. 'Relief party be with you tonight with food and medical supplies. Good luck – MacDonald RAAF.' Rescuers and survivors made rendezvous on 7 March, leaving the scene of the crash to return to Broome, after first recuperating at the Mission. The brown package had been overlooked and forgotten.

It was not to be long before the wounded pilot was subjected to persistent, sometimes hostile, in-depth questioning from the police as to the fate of the brown package. He was able to relate that, in all honesty, he never saw it again after putting it in the aircraft's safe. At that very moment at the end of March, the brown package was in the possession of a beachcomber named Jack Palmer. Inside the box was a king's ransom in diamonds. They had been sent from the Netherlands to the Dutch Indies for safe-keeping immediately before the Nazi occupation, and were almost priceless. The finder was quite blasé about his discovery, distributing diamonds as largesse to his various friends. When he surrendered himself six weeks after the plane crashed – by way of joining the Army – he handed over part of the collection, 4,571 diamonds. Over the next 12 months a further 2,025 diamonds were recovered but the combined total was less than ten per cent of the original consignment. W H Tyler estimates the present value of the lost diamonds to be in the region of A$10,000,000.

The most fortunate aviator on the day of the raid was undoubtedly Captain Jimmy Woods, flying a MacRobertson Miller Airlines Lockheed 10A. His departure on the overland route from Wyndham to Perth via Broome, was minutes before the eight Zeros machine-gunned Wyndham, causing slight damage. Jimmy Woods arrived over Broome 30 minutes after the Japanese had left. Although other aircraft trickled into Broome, Woods' ten-seater Lockheed and the Qantas *Camilla*, were pressed into a shuttle-service. Filled far beyond capacity, they evacuated the wounded, and Dutch civilians, to Port Hedland.

* * *

Lieutenant, later Brigadier John Rouse, recorded in his diary 'some remarkable examples of heroism and cowardice'. He saw a train coming landward along the jetty 'with a load of about ten or 15 dead women and children lain out on the flat cars'. The servicemen there were fully committed in getting the people out or servicing the ships. Rouse told the Dutchmen that they would have to bury their dead nationals. 'Instead, they (officials) went down to the hotels and drank beer all afternoon.' One father dug a grave in which to bury his wife and three children but most of the rest of the bodies were burned by the home guard.

*   *   *

The number of casualties had been confined to those who were killed or wounded in Roebuck Bay, the Americans aboard the Liberator, and the Dutch who had died in the Carnot Bay Incident. The total number of fatalities was impossible to determine. The Japanese had not attacked the town, obviously obeying orders and also conserving their ammunition. No one really knew how many Dutch refugees had been accommodated aboard the flying-boats. Some bodies were recovered, but others would have been swept out to sea, taken by sharks, or washed up on some remote mangrove beach. One little Dutch girl's body was found by an old Malay in the mangroves. He buried her in a shallow grave, which he tended lovingly until his secret was discovered and the body removed to join the others. The final, overall death toll was assessed to be in excess of 70.

The sense of utter helplessness, nervousness and abandonment felt by the male inhabitants of Broome, can be imagined. The last remaining white female was among the first to be evacuated after the raid. So, too, was the balance of the Dutch refugees, whose Government had chartered special aircraft from the south. The Americans had cleared the town completely in 48 hours. The airfield runway was prepared for demolition, the luggers were being systematically destroyed as part of the denial plan, the State Shipping Service announced that they would be calling no more, and the only road out of Broome not closed by the weather, was piqueted by the Army to prevent the inhabitants of Broome from overcrowding Port Hedland.

The Americans had compounded matters by persuading the nervous Australians that the Japanese always followed-up their air-attacks with amphibious landings. Worried eyes scanned the horizon. Just after the raid, an ominous smudge of smoke could be seen drawing closer and closer to the town. It proved to be the *Admiral Halstead*. Having escaped Darwin without being able to off-load all her aviation fuel, she had been two weeks at sea, over which enemy aircraft held mastery, and below which Japanese submarines had virtually a free hand. Events in Broome had made the requirement for aviation fuel superfluous, and the American freighter returned to the open sea with her dangerous cargo.

Some of the townspeople worked out a routine of evacuating the town in the morning, when the risk of air attack was at its height. Throughout the town ran a smouldering feeling of indignation and resentment that the menfolk had been abandoned. A message was sent by a town elder, chairman of the Broome Roads Board, soon after the raid, to the State Premier in Perth. 'We demand that aerial transport be sent to Broome to evacuate the civil population who desire to leave. Alternatively adequate Australian fighter protection be afforded to avoid repetition of this morning's occurrence. Road impassable.'

The Air Board was the authority for the release of scarce air assets, but they would only do so with the endorsement of the GOC in Perth. Since the Army wished to retain a fit and able labour force in the town, the necessary approval was not immediately forthcoming. The RAAF left, taking with them their own medical support. By April, the go-ahead was given for those civilians who wished to leave Broome to do so. The residue in the town amounted to a garrison of 50 infantrymen and a collection of 45, mostly elderly, Europeans who did not wish to leave.

Thus, it was that Broome became a ghost town, virtually undefended and ready for the picking. There are those who believe that the example of Broome was a manifestation which included over three-quarters of Australia's territory, involving, *in extremis*, its complete surrender without even token resistance. For those living to the north of a line drawn from Adelaide to Brisbane, there was no defence, but a denial policy known as 'Scorched Earth'.

On Saturday, 7 March, the Japanese accepted the surrender of the Netherlands Forces in the Dutch East Indies. The Japanese advance had been delayed by rearguard actions in the mountains to the north of Bandung. Inexplicably, the Japanese failed to move in and take the city after the surrender. During the course of this unexpected moratorium, efforts were made by the Dutch military staff to fly two Intelligence Captains to safety. The prevailing evacuation rules were that Dutch nationals stayed put unless authorised and nominated for repatriation.

Not unnaturally it was thought that all the aircraft capable of flying had long since gone, but someone remembered that in one of the hangars at Bandung's Andir airfield there was still a Glenn Martin, which had just been fitted with new but untested engines. The pilots, Lieutenant (later Lieutenant General) A B Wolff and Lieutenant van Erkel, cast around for a volunteer crew and as many passengers as could be accommodated. This proved to be surprisingly difficult to achieve. Nonetheless, a crew was eventually cobbled together. Unfortunately, at the surrender, all the maps had been burned along with the local currency, and Lieutenant Wolff was obliged to rely upon his niece's school atlas.

Take-off was scheduled for midnight. Most of the Dutch flying was of necessity at night to take advantage of the fact that the Japanese air force had no night fighting capability. One problem to be solved was the fact that the Glenn Martin had insufficient range to reach its destination of Broome. An auxiliary tank had therefore to be mounted inside the craft and, with the reassurance of a stranded civilian airline pilot that a useful tailwind could be expected, Wolff was advised he might just make the Australian coast. Still young, and three months married, Wolff had much to live for. All guns, parachutes, inflatable boats and the passengers' luggage were ejected from the aircraft.

After some delay, and having earlier bid farewell to his young wife who would supposedly drive the family car back to their home in Bandung, Wolff took the heavily laden Glenn Martin into the sky. The burning port of Tjilatjap provided a useful but solitary beacon for the navigator who sat in his own, cramped cockpit forward of and separated from the pilots.

Many years later, in February 1988, the sprightly, retired General Wolff, now with business interests in Indonesia, recounted his story. We had a pleasant lunch at the restaurant Het Zwaantje located on the main crossroads in the village of Soesterberg on the south side of the Royal Netherlands Airforce base. He elaborated upon why the navigator on this journey was more than usually cramped.

> When we were well out to sea, the navigator came up on the intercom to say that he was not alone up front in his cockpit. In fact, unbeknown to me, he had smuggled my wife aboard. At the time, I was both angry and dumbfounded.

Wolff had planned to beach his aircraft on the Australian coast, but luck continued to play its part and the 'plane made its landfall exactly at Broome. They saw below them the debris in the harbour and the tangled mess at the airfield. Crew and passengers were quite oblivious of the previous Japanese attacks on Broome and were not to discover that the wreckage in the harbour was predominantly the remains of Dutch aircraft until later, when they landed at Geraldtown.

The Netherlands aircraft made a safe landing at Broome, with fuel left for only a further 15-20 minutes' flying. They did indeed have the benefit of a fortuitous tail wind. When the crew left the 'plane, they looked around. The place appeared absolutely deserted. Eventually, they discovered the one available inhabitant, an old man, with whom they started to negotiate for the petrol they would need to take them away from Broome.

The elderly Australian was frightened, insisting he had to leave because the 'Japanese are not far off'. He tried to persuade the crew to go into town for their fuel because he dared not delay his escape. The old man was stopped in mid-flight by the appearance and crackle of crisp notes of the realm. Thrusting a generous wad into his pocket, he indicated to Wolff a 40 gallon drum of petrol, thrust a Kelston pump into the pilot's hand and wished him a speedy 'G'day', advising him to make for Port Hedland, a short distance along the coast to the south.

The Dutch took the old man very much at his word, believing that the Japanese might indeed return at any moment. Some of those present that morning had been caught before on the ground by Japanese Zeros. The pump was operated rapidly and with a sense of great urgency; so much so that within 30 minutes of landing, the aircraft was in the air again. Arriving over what they thought was Port Hedland, Wolff found to his dismay that the runway had been deliberately obstructed. Had his luck run out at this, the final hurdle, he wondered? Meanwhile, his industrious radio operator was hopping around the frequencies and received a directional signal from an airfield ten miles distant. They were talked-in to an extremely well-camouflaged strip which they would otherwise have missed. Luck had remained the companion of this, the very last Dutch aircraft to leave the Indies during the War.

What had bemused and riled Broome's reluctant residents, was the news which percolated through, courtesy of passing aircraft. In the *Daily News* of 4 March, they read:

> Fortunately, all women and children had been evacuated from the town and those remaining had no difficulty in taking care of themselves. The result has been that civilian damage has been slight.

The ultimate 'bottler' was to appear the next day in the *West Australian*, dated 5 March.

> The Prime Minister (Mr Curtin) today denied rumours that the loss of life at Darwin as the result of the raids on 19 February was very heavy. 'That is utterly untrue', he said. 'The same applies to raids at Broome and Wyndham yesterday. It is not in the national interest to make my statement giving details of

casualties at any particular place, as this would give valuable information to the enemy. I can assure the Australian public, however, that while losses have been incurred – whether they may be life or property – the raids were not of a kind to give that satisfaction to the enemy which he expected'.

Two days later, the *West Australian* carried a one-inch column, dateline London, of 6 March.

It was officially claimed in Tokyo today that Japanese naval 'planes which raided Broome on Tuesday destroyed 28 flying boats.

Although the number of aircraft destroyed was not exclusively flying-boats, it did appear that to glean the truth in wartime Australia, there was advantage in monitoring the enemy's reports rather than putting trust in the Government's.

*   *   *

The planned return Japanese air attack on Darwin on 4 March went ahead, when aircraft attacked the railway and airfield, setting fire to two aircraft on the ground. That attack set the pattern of continuing attacks on Darwin and its immediate area, which would last until 12 November 1943. Broome was not overlooked either, and she was to be raided on three further occasions. This escalation of Japanese activity served to convince many of those who had hung on in the north, that they ought to be heading south. There are stories from those times of prodigious and heroic efforts to achieve that aim.

On 7 April, a party of missionaries set out on a journey to escort a group of over 30 part-Aboriginal children from Croker Island, 225 kilometres north-east of Darwin, across the breadth of Australia to the cities of the south. That journey was to last two months. Cattlemen, fearful that their stock might fall into the hands of invading Japanese, started out on one of the longest drives in history. Eighty thousand head of cattle were moved from the far north, arriving in the southern cities in remarkably good condition.

Curtin did nothing in these early months to disabuse the people that the threat of invasion was real. A sense of danger and urgency had not percolated through to much more than half the population. A newspaper poll at the time revealed that only just over half of all Australians believed in the possibility of a full-scale Japanese invasion. Curtin's strident, appealing approach was vaguely reminiscent of Churchill, a man from whom he was politically poles apart and not greatly in favour. On 4 March, Curtin said:

As time passes, the enemy comes ever nearer. Darwin, Wyndham, Broome are three important strategical points in the security of Australia as a whole. I have long been impressed with the menace to the populations in our larger capital cities which this part of Australia would contribute if the enemy were able to use it as a base. Established in the north, his hitting power at the larger centres of population and of economic activity becomes all the more important.

Despite such grand announcements, there was overwhelming evidence that the Government was prepared, as a last resort, to abandon most of Australia to the enemy. Discussion of 'Scorched Earth' and the Brisbane Line were complementary factors in a course of action which, if implemented, required that the hold on all the territory to the north of the line Adelaide–Brisbane, be given up.

The 'Scorched Earth' policy was the darling of the Left, whether they were members of the Australian Communist Party or the radical elements within Curtin's Labor Party. They had become entranced by stories of the exploits of Russians with snow on their boots, fighting brave rearguard actions against the advancing Nazis. At an Aid to Russia rally, held in Sydney just after the Darwin attack, the Federal Minister for Labor, Eddie Ward, encouraged emulation of the Russians with a promise that, at the war's end, there would be 'a new social order in which you will be able to forget many of the struggles and differences of the past'. Heady stuff, but it is difficult to imagine who would be swayed by the unlikely logic enshrined in a policy of scorched earth. Douglas Lockwood's book, *Australia's Pearl Harbour*, contains this illuminating little paragraph from Darwin:

> Among the first to leave were some of the officials of North Australia Workers' Union in the union truck. For several weeks they had been advocating a scorched earth policy in the event of invasion. An Official War History investigator was told: 'The only scorching done by these chaps was along the road to Adelaide River'.

Where the logic was found wanting was in the mismatch between the Russian and Australian models. The Russians withdrew in heavy snow along their lines of communication, rebuilding reserves, depending on the elements to reduce the fighting efficiency of their enemy, trading space for time prior to launching their own counter-moves with resources drawn from their own national assets. Australia had few reserves and, of the fighting qualities of those soldiers he had seen, MacArthur said on at least two occasions, 'these soldiers will not fight'.

In reality, the policy had not been thought through. What was to be the next recommended step, for example, for those living on the coastal strips beyond the Brisbane Line who denied the enemy their possessions and property? The option seemed to be either to position themselves on the safe side of the line, or to head into an interior, scorched or drowned according to the season, with a prospect of no food, and either too little or too much water.

The resurrection of a Brisbane Line concept can be laid squarely at the doors of the Australian generals, General Sir Ivan Mackay and Lieutenant General Sir Vernon Sturdee. They took the core recommendation from the Monash Report, extending the line of defence northwards to embrace Brisbane, fast becoming the home of the United States' Forces. The evidence is irrefutable that the Brisbane Line strategy did exist. It is equally clear that, as a worst case contingency plan, it was loosely supported among the hierarchy of both the two main political parties. Few could disagree that Australia could not be strong everywhere. That it was to become an extremely hot political issue, was due in no small part to the inflammatory activities of Eddie Ward in the lead-up to the 21 August 1943 General Election.

So incensed were the previous members of the UAP-Country Party Government by Ward's politically damaging allegations of the existence of a strategy of abandonment, that they were able to force the convening of a Royal Commission to investigate the matter. Ironically, the Royal Commissioner was Mr Justice Lowe, who had presided over the investigation into the Darwin *débâcle*. The Commission raised more heat than light. The key contingency plan, which Ward insisted had been removed from its official file, was judged probably to have never existed. Any further progress that the Commission might have achieved, was checked by Ward, who stood on his parliamentary privilege, refusing to answer any questions. Doubtless Prime Minister Curtin was relieved, for later he was to admit that, at the time when the Japanese threat appeared at its most dangerous, the Labor Party, too, had examined the feasibilities of the Brisbane Line strategy.

The Brisbane Line concept was put to rest after MacArthur's arrival in Australia. To what degree this re-appraisal was due to MacArthur is difficult to determine for, in studying the man, it is at times difficult to separate the myth from reality. Allegedly, he arrived to find a depressed, defeatist and fatalistic nation in search, or at least in need, of inspirational leadership. MacArthur's conduct in Australia was to be determined by a happy compromise between what was best for the United States and best for MacArthur. Sitting back in the south-east corner of Australia was hardly likely to achieve the United States' overall expansionist aims for the region or, for that matter, for MacArthur to honour his pledge to the Philippines that he would return. 'We shall make the fight for Australia in New Guinea', he declared. With the infusion of troops, capital and equipment that followed the man, the defences of the vacuous north were to be transformed for the better.

Whether or not the Brisbane Line was a rational, valid plan to deal with extreme, last-ditch circumstances, is not relevant to the situation which was allowed to prevail in Darwin, Broome and Wyndham. It was the very existence of the plan which meant that resources, admittedly in short supply, were not put at risk in areas likely to be overrun. MacArthur's assessment that the Japanese would not invade but rather conduct a series of raids, proved to be accurate. The Japanese did not come to Australia in force. Those who did arrive, came as defeated servicemen caught by the turning tide of Allied victories. The vanquished Japanese soldiers were gathered up in dribs and drabs, to be consigned to a prisoner-of-war camp in a small New South Wales farming town by the name of Cowra.

COWRA

4. Cowra

Cowra is an unremarkable town. It lies in the so-called Golden West Region of New South Wales, 366 kilometres west of Sydney. As the regional name suggests, it owes its livelihood to agricultural activities and supports a population of 12,000. The town's origins can be traced to the 1830s when Arthur Rankin and James Sloan brought their cattle to graze the rich grasslands of the Lachlan river. Gold-strikes at Young and Grenfell attracted would-be miners by the thousand, crossing the river at the point where the town was to be established. The first pioneers heard from the numerous Aborigines living along the banks of the Lachlan that the area was known to them as Cowra. Cowra is the Aboriginal word for rocks; the grey, granite rocks which overlook the present town like random knuckles protruding from sparse, tree-lined hillocks.

The ordinariness of the place veils the truth that Cowra is the site of an Australian Second World War battlefield. It is the only location on mainland Australia where members of opposing armies fought one another in a full-blooded battle. The events which occurred here differed from those of Darwin and Broome, which were characterised by strong, surprise attacks against weak, unprepared defences.

On the morning of 5 August 1944, over 900 Japanese prisoners attempted to break out of their prisoner-of-war camp situated 3 kilometres north-east of Cowra. This action surpassed that of the 'Great Escape' from *Stalag Luft 3*, Silesia, in March 1944 in terms of the number of participants, fervour, ferocity, and in the total casualties. When the break-out had run its course, 344 prisoners had succeeded in escaping confinement, but in the débris, the fatalities included 231 Japanese, and four Australian soldiers stabbed or bludgeoned to death. Two of those Australian soldiers were to receive the belated, posthumous award of the George Cross.

At the end of the war, the camp was dismantled. Very little evidence of it ever having been there remains. A cairn has been erected to mark the spot where the main escape occurred and, beyond a low barbed-wire fence, the concrete foundations of the old huts can be found among the grass. Of the original camp, the only really visible evidence is two pillars in Binni Creek Road, marking the former entrance to the camp. They now serve as a memorial to the four Australian soldiers who died. Both pillars stand incongruously, now overwhelmed by a housing estate, just as the men they commemorate were overwhelmed by the fanatical Japanese prisoners they were guarding.

In 1941, the year the prisoner-of-war camp was first established, Cowra was a much more closely-knit town. The population was approximately 4,000, of which perhaps one quarter supported the new two-compound prison camp as well as the nearby recruit training facilities. The first prisoners were Italians. They were easy-going, good-natured, unashamed men who, when confronted with the decision between a pointless death and living, found no difficulty within their national ethos in selecting the latter course. They had surrendered in the Western Desert by the battalion. In Cowra, they became a happy-go-lucky and popular enemy, luxuriating in a climate not dissimilar to their own Bella Italia. So trusted did they become, that they were frequently sent off as live-in help on the local farmsteads. Occasionally, when administration failed and they had to make their own way back to camp, they would bang on the double gates, demanding to be let into the prison. These were early, heady days in a camp designed to cater for docile incumbents content to see the war out in safe and not unreasonable conditions. Japan was not yet at war, but her plans for the pre-emptive attack on Pearl Harbor were already well advanced.

The ultimate decision as to whether Japan should, or should not, go to war, rested with the Imperial Japanese Navy. As a Service, they were not as mesmerised as the Army by the sense of Japan's manifest destiny in Asia. Their attitude was more cautious, for they were acutely aware of the combat power available to the United States; ten times that of Japan. As late as the autumn of 1941, the Naval General Staff pleaded with the Minister for the Navy to state publicly that there was no prospect of winning a war against the United States and her allies. He responded lamely: 'Having boasted of our invincible fleet, we can not now insist upon compromise and say that we are unable to fight. We would lose face everywhere.'

It is history that the navy capitulated to the majority view, and took to the task in hand with such commitment that it might have appeared that they had been supportive from the outset. Despite the brilliance of his Pearl Harbor planning, Admiral Yamamoto confided to a colleague:

If we are ordered to fight the United States, we might be able to score a run-away victory and hold our own for six months or a year. But in the second year, the Americans will increase their strength and it will be very difficult for us to fight on with any prospect of final victory.

It was, for Japan, a tragedy that they did not heed Yamamoto's publicly-expressed reservations before embarking upon a course of action founded on gross optimism and miscalculation. The attack on Pearl Harbor, while an undoubted strategic victory, was nonetheless self-defeating. No action was quite so guaranteed to mobilise the, until then lackadaisical, American public into a united, howling body of protest aimed at avenging Japanese infamy.

The United States and her allies required just over a year to turn the tide against Japan. The bombing of Japanese cities, including Tokyo, was an indication of what was to come, followed closely by the naval victories of the Coral Sea and Midway. The Battle of Midway, 4-5 June 1942, had been a stunning victory, which saw the four carriers responsible for the attack on Darwin consigned to the bottom of the sea. With them went Rear-Admiral Yamaguchi, the proponent of the surprise attack.

The key land battle which confirmed the change in Japan's war fortune was the Battle of Guadalcanal, which ended on 7 February 1943, and initiated the first of successive Japanese withdrawals. The concurrent, dogged Australian fighting along the Kokoda Track to Buna, showed conclusively that well-led, well-motivated soldiers with high morale, could defeat the Japanese. What is more, these two actions produced a new phenomenon; significant numbers of Japanese prisoners-of-war.

One important constituent in the Japanese concept for success against the Allies was the supremely simplistic idea that, by inflicting upon the members of the Western Alliance unacceptably heavy casualties, the stage would be reached where they would sue for peace. This plan, therefore, asked a great deal of the soldier, sailor and airman in the relatively small Imperial Japanese Services.

The ethos of the ultimate sacrifice, fighting to the death, was widely aired by the Japanese media, stressing the undesirability of surrender, being something quite foreign and contrary to the Japanese Way. The surrender of large numbers of Russians at Port Arthur in 1905, and of the Commonwealth Forces in Singapore, amazed the Japanese because it was the very antithesis of their own Military Field Code. That part dealing with surrender read:

> He who knows shame is strong and should at all times endeavour to keep before him the honour of his homeland and live up to what is expected of him. Rather than live and bear the shame of imprisonment by the enemy, he should die and avoid leaving a dishonourable name.

Almost always the Japanese serviceman honoured the code, either by saving his last bullet for himself, or by making a brave, useless, suicidal charge towards his enemy's guns. Unfortunately, such matters are rarely quite so tidily cut and dried.

The first of the Japanese prisoners-of-war was one of ten submariners involved in the midget submarine attack on Pearl Harbor. Despite the crew's bravery, the five submarines failed to inflict any damage at all upon the United States' fleet.* The nine who died, however, were elevated and revered as War Gods at home. The survivor, the unfortunate Ensign Kazuo Sakamaki, was ignored. In becoming a prisoner, he was disgraced: a non-person who had ceased to be of further relevance. From the outset, the Japanese authorities had set their standard.

Included in the Allies' war training package for their servicemen was instruction on the Geneva Convention, which defines the rights and status of prisoners-of-war. This training prepared Allied servicemen for the event of their capture, and emphasised, for example, that all they were obliged to reveal was their number, rank and name.

Japan had signed the 1929 Geneva Convention but, under intense pressure from the powerful military lobby, failed to ratify the Convention in 1934. The military had seen in this international agreement, similarities with other contemporary legislation aimed at limiting Japan's progress along the path to her ultimate destiny. In consequence, when Japanese did become prisoners-of-war, they were totally unprepared for the experience. They had not been briefed by their superiors for a contingency not imagined likely to arise. When they reached their camps, they were to be totally unsupported by their uncaring Government.

The Australians were conscious that a gap existed in the Japanese prisoners' knowledge of their rights and status. To that end, an explanatory leaflet was distributed to each captive while undergoing his essential incubation in transit camps. At first the leaflets were reas-

---

* The team was trained by Lieutenant Matsuo who conducted a more profitable miniature submarine attack in Sydney Harbour, May 1942. An attack, incidentally, which caused more alarm and commotion than the attack on Darwin. Matsuo did not return.

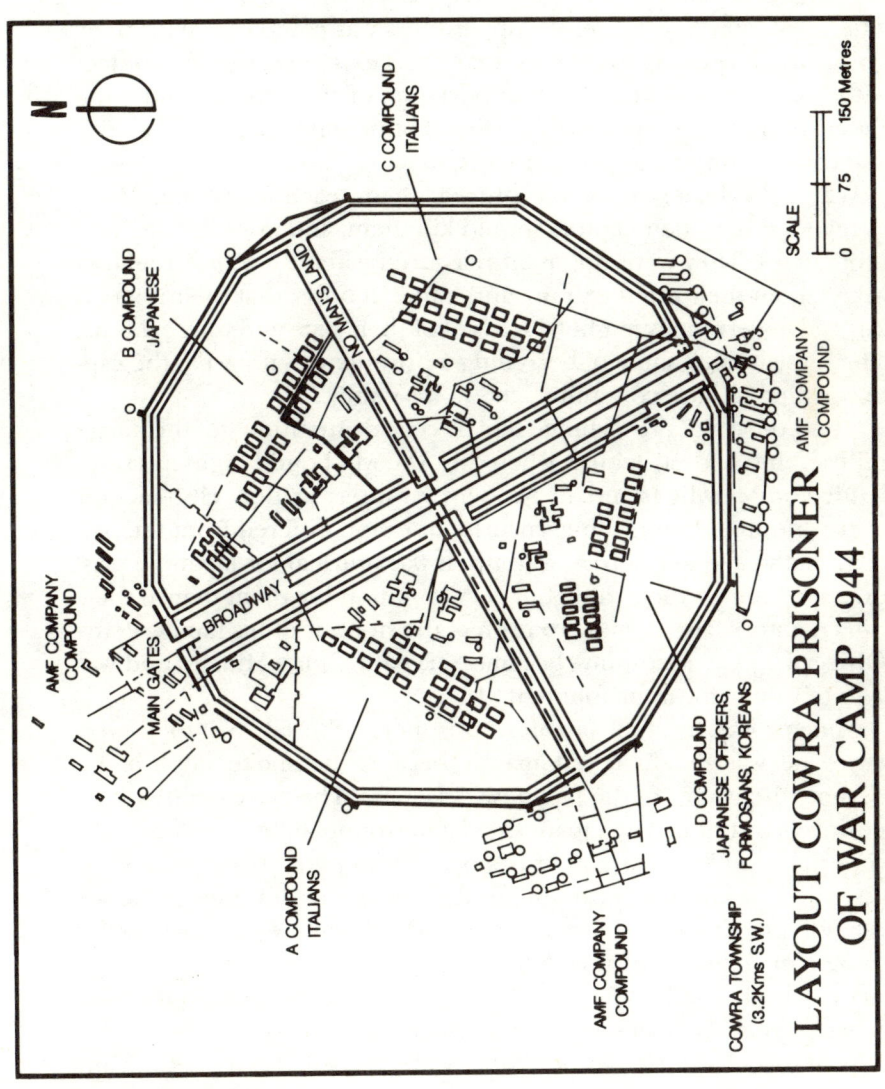

LAYOUT COWRA PRISONER
OF WAR CAMP 1944

suring, but their value was diluted once the prisoner arrived at his final place of internment.

The Italians in the adjoining compounds were in receipt of Red Cross parcels and letters from home. The Japanese had none of this. Their isolation and sense of hopelessness was complete. With their government refusing to acknowledge their existence, with no contact with loved ones at home, the importance of the support and comradeship that developed within groups of prisoners was to be a critical, contributory factor to future events.

When the Japanese were captured, their reactions varied. Many demanded that their captors should kill them, and most had suicidal tendencies. They were not at all reassured when their interrogators asked them their number, rank and name in order that their next-of-kin and government might be advised of their state and whereabouts. The unbearable shame of becoming a prisoner was not what the captive wished to have communicated to his family.

After the pilot Toyoshima had received attention to the facial injuries he had sustained when his Darwin-bound fighter crash-landed on Melville Island, he was sent for interrogation. His reaction to the 'number, rank, name' surprise question differed from the pattern that was to develop. As a trend, it was unusual for Japanese prisoners to change their rank, but very common for them to give their interrogators false names. To protect the honour of his family, Petty-Officer Hajime Toyoshima became Sergeant Tadao Minami and was sent to Cowra for imprisonment.

Minami was the first Japanese prisoner to be taken into Cowra. Since he was the first, but mainly because he spoke English, he became the leader of the Japanese prisoners. The early months were positively tranquil. The Japanese prisoner population increased only very slowly with the arrival of the occasional pilot. These men were essentially individuals with little in the way of unit loyalties or corporate identity. It was not difficult for the first Japanese to slide into the *laissez faire* lethargy of the Italians, whose accommodation they initially shared. The first favourable impression of the behaviour of the Japanese prisoners-of-war was therefore misleading and fostered a false sense of security, to be dramatically dispelled once significant numbers of Army prisoners arrived.

The steady influx of Japanese prisoners from early 1943 prompted a reorganisation of Number Twelve Prisoner-of-War Group, from a two- to a four-compound camp. Nothing was done to upgrade security or to differentiate between levels of risk emanating from the totally different national groups. Each separate 17 acre site was designed to accommodate up to 1,000 prisoners. The whole was enclosed by a 12 sided perimeter, enclosing an almost circular area.

The Group Headquarters were situated on the high ground to the western side of the four camps. The Group Commandant and Commanding Officer of 22 Australian Garrison Battalion, raised specifically to guard the camp, was a First World War veteran and cavalry officer, Lieutenant-Colonel M A Brown. Under him were his company commanders, double-hatted to perform the duties as camp commandants for each of the four camps.

At the time of the break-out, Compounds A and C held Italian other-ranks, Compound B under Major R Ramsay held 1,104 Japanese other-ranks, while Compound D consisted of Japanese officers and Koreans and Formosans. The composition of the latter Compound was a strange mix since, under normal circumstances, the Koreans and Formosans were recruited by the Japanese in the Imperial Work Force to perform general or menial duties. In theory, this released more Japanese for martial employment.

A 50-metre wide and 750-metre long thoroughfare ran the length of the camp, dividing Compounds B and C on the eastern side from Compounds A and D on the west. During silent hours, this roadway was bathed in electric light, giving rise to its name of Broadway. Deep storm drains had been dug parallel to the roadway to take away the water which accumulated in the camp area from the surrounding low hills. At each end of Broadway were heavy wooden double gates. A rough pathway, approximately ten metres wide, divided the compound into its established quarters by bisecting Broadway. On each side of this pathway, known as 'No Man's Land', were the security fences. Within each compound was a cluster of some 20 accommodation huts enclosed by three barbed-wire fences ten metres apart. Each fence was just under two metres high, supported by posts three metres apart carrying half-a-dozen lines of barbed-wire on each side of the fence posts. Between the outer and inner barbed-wire fences was a tangle of wire to a height of almost two metres. On the inside of the middle fence were three coils of dannert concertina wire, with a further coil overhanging at the top. At strategic points outside the camp perimeter were six nine-metre high towers mounting light automatic weapons.

The northern and southern wooden double gates of Broadway were the sole means of access to the perimeter. Each of the four compounds had their own individual double, and outer and inner gates, located at the centre of Broadway. The guards' accommodation was outside and close to the two Broadway gates. The 'Northern Area', on slightly rising ground, was the company lines for those soldiers guarding A and B Compounds, while the 'Southern Area' provided the sleeping quarters and accommodation for those guarding C and D Compounds.

The number of Japanese captured in proportion to those killed was probably less than one per cent. Of those who arrived at Cowra, many were in a poor state, having been wounded or rendered unconscious prior to capture – not that these were mitigating circumstances. Because they were unaware of their entitlement, under the Geneva Convention, to fair and humane treatment, they were surprised by their handling by the Australians. Since they were regarded by their own kind as being as good as dead, and because they were led to believe that if they were caught they would suffer torture and indignities, they expected nothing less. That the Australians did not resort to heavy-handedness and agreed to all but the most extreme of the Japanese demands, led the prisoners to believe their captors to be soft and beneath contempt.

The essential reason for the disdain on the Japanese side and the benevolent indifference of the 'Digger' guards, had much to do with their representing different generations. Colonel Brown's men were, for the most part, of that age-group too young to follow the call to the First World War and too old for the Second. There were some younger, medically down-graded soldiers at Cowra, but it was usual to find the private soldiers in their early- to mid-40s.

To the young, eager, energetic Japanese ideologists, their captors were not warriors, but a non-combatant Dad's Army. From the behaviour of their young Officer Corps, arrogant, petulant, even childish, they needed and would have respected a strong, parental-style discipline. Unfortunately, the guards were not permitted to be too firm with the Japanese. Appeasement was the order of the day, due to a fundamental misconception of inter-relationships in the Japanese Armed Forces. In the compound, a gradual testing of the limits of Australian latitude began. There were complaints about the food, demands for separate national days to be set aside, refusal to work. The compound authorities remained largely acquiescent, with the rather inexplicable exception that they refused to allow the prisoners to drop shaving from their morning ablutions.

Australia obeyed and pursued the letter of the Geneva Convention, even taking their generosity to extremes. The prisoners demanded far more food than they could possibly eat. The surpluses, they quite simply buried and forgot. In the strange logic of the prisoners, this was their contribution to their nation's war effort.

When the Swiss representatives of the International Red Cross visited Cowra, they found nothing contrary to the Convention, and even informal talks with the prisoners gave the impression that everything was in order. It was important to the Australian authorities that nothing adverse should arise from these inspection visits. The sensitivity was due to the conviction that any criticism of the handling of the Japanese prisoners would be seized upon by Japan to exert reprisals upon the Australians in their hands. Herein lay a misconception as to Japan's attitude to her own nationals in prisoner-of-war camps. Confirmation can be found in the Army Report which investigated the break-out: 'The slightest incident, if not handled properly or reported correctly, was likely to be used by the enemy as a lever for enforcing restrictions on Allied prisoners-of-war in its camps'. It is fair to add that this was a common misconception, shared by Britain in particular.

At the time that the Japanese prisoners were indulging in relative luxury, there were 21,000 Australians in Japanese hands, and a total of 46,000 Allied prisoners-of-war were suffering savage deprivation while building the Burma–Siam Railway. There was little scope remaining for the Japanese to treat their captives more inhumanely. It was Japanese policy, promulgated by Tojo, to treat their prisoners according to their own ideology and, in this matter, commandants were given a free hand to impose discipline as they saw fit.

The Japanese could not appreciate that the Allied prisoners did not regard their patriotism or loyalty to be in question through their having been captured. Their duty was to regain their own lines if and when a suitable opportunity arose, but not by suicidal gestures. They were deprived of their mandatory rights under the Geneva Convention, firstly because it was not recognised by Japan, and secondly, the prospect of counter-reprisals upon their own nationals was, to the Japanese, a matter of monumental indifference. Even in the camps of Japan's Axis allies, 96 per cent of the prisoners survived their imprisonment. Of the Allies held by the Japanese, over one quarter died in the camps and, of those that were released at war's end, many had a severely reduced life-expectancy.

Until August 1944, homeland Australia had no Second World War tradition of great escapes, or even attempts at great escapes. The options open to Australia's prisoners were not as many as those in the better-known European model. Within the confines of Europe, there was greater opportunity for Allied prisoners-of-war to regain their own side, crossing into neutral or home territory aided by an in-place resistance movement. Would-be Japanese escapees would not have fitted into what was then essentially a white Australia. In addition, the geography of island-Australia could not have been better suited to frustrate the attempts of would-be escapees.

The official Army Report of the break-out lists only two other main events of importance ranking with that of the escape at Cowra. The first concerned tunnelling operations of prisoners-of-war, and the second was the not-widely-reported shooting of German prisoners at Murchison, Victoria, in September 1942. There had been, however, a successful escape by a Cowra prisoner in April 1943.

The three rows of head-high barbed-wire fences had posed no problem to the truculent Lieutenant Naka. However, whatever his motive for escaping, that had been the easy part. As he headed east-ward towards the coast, the headlights of an oncoming vehicle picked out his diminutive, red-clad figure. A warning shot from the com-pound sounded the alarm to assemble the pursuing 'hounds', while the Japanese scurried across the open farm country, trying to put as much distance as possible between him and his pursuers.

Naka was not long at large, but a number of important lessons did arise. The pointlessness of the exercise could not have been lost on the escapee, who nonetheless basked in an aura of adulation and hero-worship. When he was captured he asked to be killed, but this was understandably declined. Naka's escape had, in any event, high-lighted the shortage of weapons available, both to defend the com-pounds and to be sent out with patrols. The camp's equipment table had been criminally neglected. All the Quartermaster had on his inventory were a few outdated Lewis and Hotchkiss light machine-guns and one rifle to share among each of the lorry-borne patrols sent out after Naka.

If, therefore, there was little by way of precedent available in Australia to forewarn of the impending, massive break-out attempt, there had been an episode in New Zealand in February 1943 which, although not entirely comparable, nonetheless held grave portents of what could happen. Featherstone prisoner-of-war camp, near Wellington, was established in September 1942 on a First World War training camp site. It was divided into two compounds, one of which held 500 Koreans and Formosans of the Imperial Work Force, cap-tured en masse at Guadalcanal and the second, Number Two

Compound, contained mostly naval personnel, officers, NCOs and other-ranks. Communication through the rank structure was therefore easy, unlike in Cowra where the officers used semaphore to signal instructions to NCOs and soldiers.

The 500 members of the Imperial Work Force took no part in the disturbances and will not be discussed further. The trouble developed slowly but persistently in the Number Two Compound. Yet again, there is clear evidence that the Japanese did not understand that they were being treated in accordance with the Geneva Convention. The handling of the prisoners by the authorities was impeccable, responding fully, for example, to the recommendations of the Red Cross Inspectorate by providing the prisoners with games, films and amusements.

The source of the Japanese lack of amusement was summed up after the event by their leader, Sub-Lieutenant Adachi:

> Many of our comrades have died bravely in battle. We have disgraced them by becoming prisoners-of-war and for this reason many of us thought that, although we were prisoners-of-war, it was totally against our Japanese tradition to work for the enemy.

The work at which the Japanese balked was quite legitimate and included attendance at fatigue parades and maintaining the camp in good order. The prisoners believed that compulsory labour was a measure adopted by the captors to emphasise the stigma, shame and humiliation of those who had transgressed their Military Field Code by permitting themselves to be taken as prisoners-of-war.

Arguments over work practices continued, often heatedly, while concurrently a series of plots would arise, as though the prisoners were determined to take some kind of overt action in order to ameliorate the shame of imprisonment. One plot dreamed up by the sailors was to indulge in mass *harakiri*, with the officers taking the lead. Understandably, the officers demurred and, fearing their lives to be at risk, had the militants removed to a separate compound. It was at this point that the leadership swayed into the hands of the senior NCOs.

The origin of the Featherstone disturbance, beginning on 23 February, involved the senior NCOs and some ratings. The former objected to the work being conducted by the ratings just outside the compound wire, and ordered the latter to stop what they were doing and return inside the compound. The Commandant, quite rightly believing his authority to be at risk of being usurped, had the three

NCOs concerned brought before him. Their surly, insolent attitude did not help his demeanour, and the Japanese were given three days to 'get their act together' or face the consequences. The consequences were, the isolation of the NCOs from the ratings. There is no doubt that this ultimatum, the threat of the break-up of established groups, was the cause of the impending violence – as it would be also in Cowra.

Matters came to a head on 25 February when the NCOs refused to supply work parties. This time, Sub-Lieutenant Adachi was in the compound, seemingly to regain control of the situation and to regain face. Adachi refused the Adjutant's orders to provide work parties and, further, insisted that the prisoners would not muster until he had had an opportunity to discuss the matter with the Commandant. The confrontation developed within the compound whereby neither party appeared to be in a position to back away from predictable disaster. The prisoners picked up rocks, jostled the guards, and when a warning shot was fired by the Adjutant over Adachi's head, the guards were stoned. A second shot was fired at Adachi, who had put himself in the unenviable position of not being able to compromise for fear of losing face with his assembled subordinates. When that shot hit him in the shoulder, it was the unintended signal for the threatening prisoners to erupt into a wild riot, attacking the guards with rocks. In a short period, 48 prisoners were killed and 63 wounded.

The repercussions are of interest. The New Zealand Prime Minister, Peter Fraser, sent a personal SECRET signal to London, to his Ambassador in Washington, and to Prime Minister Curtin. The signal gave an outline of the previous day's events and sought procedural advice from Britain. The British response encouraged New Zealand to remain resolute and not to appear guilty with regard to the shootings but also, significantly, suggested that the Swiss International Red Cross delegate should be warned to play down the event so as not to initiate a Japanese backlash among Allied prisoners-of-war. The Swiss acted as the Protecting Power, overseeing Japanese interests both in New Zealand and Australia.

The ensuing Inquiry was meticulously conducted. None of the New Zealand troops was found to be culpable but, in a mealy-mouthed statement, the ultimate blame was placed on Adachi and his immediate supporters, with the caveat that this finding was based on European standards and subject to Japan's commitment to a Convention that she had not ratified. Japan made a token response in September, threatening to use armed force against Allied prisoners but, after a short exchange of memoranda the event was forgotten. Despite New Zealand's meticulous efforts to keep the Commonwealth nations and Washington fully informed as to the origins and outcome at Featherstone, some of the lessons learned were not applied at Cowra. The grapevine proved to be very effective because it was not too long before the Cowra prisoners heard of the atonement their comrades had achieved in New Zealand.

An indication that the war was not going well for Japan was reflected in the number of army prisoners collecting at Cowra. In the year leading up to the escape, the strength had doubled with the greatest gains being from March 1944 onwards. The effect of the massive influx of army men was to influence the inter-prisoner relationships. The soldiers of B Compound held little respect for the airmen, and saw no justification in them retaining the camp leadership purely on the basis of the length of time they had been at Cowra. Minami was an exception. He was held in respect, and his command of English meant that he controlled the communication between prisoner and captor. In the end, it was decided to elect a new leadership by ballot. As a result, the new elected camp leader was a veteran army Sergeant-Major Akira Kanazawa. He was assisted by an army deputy, and the third-in-command slot was given to the indispensable Minami.

The Army was more militant, more aggressive than the Air Force, and their arrival in strength heralded a discernible increase in tension. The staff continued about their duties patiently and remained acquiescent. The changing climate was most certainly not due to ill-treatment of the prisoners by the guards. Nevertheless, there was an air of restlessness and impatience, rather like a herd of cattle unsettled by the threat of storm. The demands of the prisoners increased, as did the incidence of refusals to obey orders and to work. A complete breakdown and confrontation now appeared to be inevitable.

Takeo Matsumoto was the assumed Japanese name of one of the Korean workers. He arrived at Cowra on 12 March 1944 and, being an instinctively inquisitive man, happened to overhear the induction briefing being given to recent arrivals by the Japanese camp leader. He heard of the prisoners' contingency plan, to be implemented at a suitable occasion, to break out of Cowra. For a while Matsumoto harboured his secret, but all the while he was to be niggled by concern of the effects of the Japanese break-out upon their Korean lackeys. He held no love for the Japanese, and saw no reason why the members of the Imperial Work Force should be punished as a result of

Japanese initiatives which quite obviously did not include them. Matsumoto continued to keep his counsel until he was interviewed by Intelligence for having been out-of-bounds in the Italian compound. The interrogators were soon satisfied that Matsumoto had not been about dark or devious deeds, and recommended that he should receive the standard punishment for transgressing the camp rules – ten days' detention.

When the Korean came out of detention on 2 June 1944, he had obviously reflected upon his situation and asked to be interviewed again by his former interpreter. 'I have', he said, 'more information to pass on'. On the second occasion, the day after his release from confinement, he was interrogated by a Captain from the Allied Translation and Intelligence Section at Brisbane. What the Korean had to say caused the Captain's face to show the concern he felt as the question and answering session enabled him to place before Lieutenant-Colonel Brown a short, accurate analysis of the Japanese prisoners' intentions.

The contents of the report surprised Brown. When Major Ramsay, responsible for B Compound, was called in to discuss the matter, he dismissed the intelligence report as groundless. The wiser, more senior officer disagreed, and felt that there must be grains of truth in the Intelligence summary before him. There was to be none of the prevarication which had been such a feature of Darwin. The report confirmed the existence of a break-out plan. The plan was for a mass break-out, at an appropriate time, which would overcome the obstacles in a manner already predetermined. The ultimate objective of the prisoners was the nearby recruit training camp, where it was intended to overwhelm the raw soldiers, steal their weapons, and inflict heavy loss upon the Australian troops. Brown sent a copy of the report by priority mail up the chain-of-command to his superior headquarters in Sydney.

The Japanese bided their time, waiting for the right opportunity. Their resurgent interest in fitness-training was noted by their guards. A request for round-shaped stones to mark out a running track was declined. Something had been learned from Featherstone, yet requests for additional gardening tools were approved. Bearing in mind the revelation, after the events at Featherstone, of an array of hand-made weapons, this was not the time to improve the Japanese armoury at Cowra. Surprisingly, having been forewarned, the authorities made no attempt either to search the huts for illicit weapons, or to remove implements that could be fashioned into weapons.

* * *

On 6 June, Lieutenant-Colonel Brown's telephone rang. He was summoned urgently to the office of the Adjutant-General in Sydney. When asked what credence he attached to Matsumoto's assertion, Brown said he believed the report to be factually correct, although it was not possible to guess when the actual break-out would be attempted. When the General enquired what additional increments he needed, Brown asked for two Vickers machine-guns, Brens, Owen guns, and more rifles. It would appear that he did not ask for reinforcements. That night, the two promised Vickers machine-guns and some additional Lewis guns already held in stock, were consigned to Cowra.

The fundamental problem in applying prophylactic fire to the Cowra camp layout, was that it was circular. Machine-guns are ideally-suited to fire alongside and parallel to obstacles. Thus, in order to achieve the best results, straight lines are needed, not fences arcing away from the fixed lines of the medium machine-guns. The siting of the guns had to take account of the fact that the camp was only 800 metres across and, given the extending beaten-zone of automatic fire, own troops and non-combative prisoners would be as much, if not more, at risk as intending escapees. All this had to be taken in to account, but the problem was simplified, in that the authorities had only to focus their attention on the threat emanating from B Compound.

Gradually, almost imperceptibly, the camp security was tightened. In B Compound, the guards were told to increase their vigilance, but they were not told of the existing Japanese escape plans. It would be stretching the imagination if they had not discerned that something out of the ordinary was afoot. A new, three-man guard post was established in the centre of Broadway, all ranks were told to sleep with their weapons, and plans were made for the issue of 50 rounds of ball ammunition to each man. The collective warning measures in the event of a mass break-out had an element of fail-safe provision, depending on the firing of two rifle-shots, the sounding of the siren, and the firing of three red Verey lights. The latter was designed to alert the nearby recruit training camp which, it will be remembered, was the intended target of the prisoners. They were to acknowledge the red flares by firing three greens.

By August, Cowra camp was overcrowded. B Compound, designed to accommodate 1,000 prisoners, now had a complement of 1,104. It was clear that transfers had to be made. The Intelligence recommen-

119

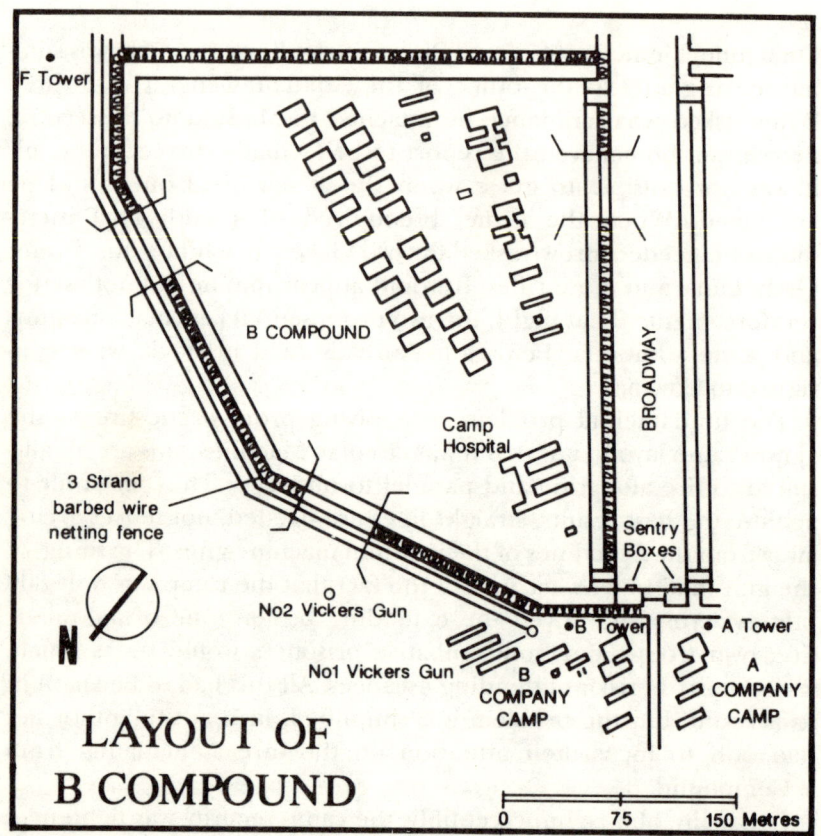

F Tower

B COMPOUND

BROADWAY

Camp
Hospital

3 Strand
barbed wire
netting fence

No2 Vickers Gun

Sentry
Boxes

N

No1 Vickers Gun

B Tower

A Tower

B
COMPANY
CAMP

A
COMPANY
CAMP

LAYOUT OF
B COMPOUND

0   75   150 **Metres**

dation argued that, since most of the trouble-makers were NCOs, there was logic in separating out the private soldiers and removing them from the influence of their NCOs. In absolute secrecy, lists were drawn up of 700 private soldiers to be sent to the camp at Hay, 290 kilometres to the west. In this camp there were also Italians, but the Japanese there, mostly merchant sailors and the pearl-divers from Broome and Darwin, were hardly militant. The authorities in Cowra were well-aware of the time-bomb that they were building and of the effect the release of this news would have upon the inmates.

The arrival of an escort party of 50 guards from Hay on 3 August, confirmed that a transfer was imminent. If the news had been leaked to the Japanese, or they had put two-and-two together, they gave no outward indication. There is some debate as to whether Lieutenant-Colonel Brown was obliged to give the Japanese notice of the impending move. It is apparent that he did believe that to be the case, and this is supported by the provisions of the Geneva Convention, which rule that prisoners-of-war who are to be transferred, have to be advised officially, in advance, of their destination. If Australia was to maintain her impeccable record in complying with the Convention, irrespective of Japan's position, then it appears Lieutenant-Colonel Brown had no alternative. What he was about to tell the prisoners was the trigger which had initiated the Featherstone troubles.

After lunch on Friday, 4 August 1944, the three compound leaders, Sergeant-Major Kanazawa, his deputy, Sergeant-Major Masao Kojuna and Minami, were called to Major Ramsay's office. The official account has it that a nominal roll was handed to the group, with the statement that all the prisoners included thereon, all below the rank of Lance-Corporal, would be transferred to Hay on Monday, 7 August 1944. It is alleged that after Minami examined the list of intended transferees, he remarked: 'Very bad business. Why can't we all go?' Major Ramsay declined to enter into a discussion, explaining that the decision had been made at superior headquarters.

In his book, *Die Like the Carp*, Harry Gordon produces evidence from Sergeant-Major Kanazawa, corroborated by the Australian interpreter then present, that there was no mention of the all-important rank separation during the interview with Major Ramsay. It is alleged that the Japanese discovered this accidentally by themselves, later in the day, and took grave exception to having being misled. The inference is that, had due regard been given to an understanding of Japanese ideology and better communications, the events at Cowra need never have occurred. A contrary view could equally be elucidated, that the break-out plan existed, the prisoners' consciences required that they do something to atone for their shame, that weaponry was already stowed in place and, had the proposed move not been the actual trigger, another future pretext would have been used before the events ran their inevitable course.

Sergeant-Major Kanazawa called a meeting of hut leaders for early that evening, with the aim of discussing the implementation of the break-out plan that very night. It was a Friday night, the traditional night for soldiers everywhere to have a good time on the town. The weather forecast promised a clear, starlit night with a touch of ground-frost. In the Australian camp there was a general conviction that the Japanese would only attempt a break-out in misty or foggy conditions. Of the three nights available to them, it appeared certain that this Friday night was not one. It seems difficult for western minds to fathom that, for a group which had decided that the time to die had come, the conditions most favourable were those pertinent to that Friday night. Kanazawa was to insist that the prospect of inflicting death and injury on the Australians was of only secondary importance. Their aim was to die, to release themselves from the dishonour that they had brought upon themselves. Despite the increase in tension, no reinforcement of guards occurred, and the two Vickers machine-guns were left unmanned.

The preliminary meeting split up prior to the evening meal. Hut leaders were told to discuss the matter with the occupants of their hut and to report back at 8 pm. Kanazawa had instructed each of the departing leaders that there had to be unanimity; it was to be all or nothing.

As each hut held its debate, it became evident that there was hesitancy in some areas. Where doubts existed, a few of the representatives were sent back to Kanazawa's hut with the message that if the majority supported the plan, then the doves would show their solidarity. Unanimity was essential, and the final decision to go was clearly the majority opinion. Kanazawa once again dispersed the hut leaders back to their accommodation to make the necessary preparation while the inner clique of leaders got down to the detailed planning. In the huts, weapons were removed from hiding places and combustibles were gathered with which to fire the buildings. The blankets were held centrally, for they were required to drape over the series of low wire fences. Similarly, gloves, particularly baseball gloves, were in demand in order to handle the barbed-wire. As a courtesy, the Japanese officers were informed but neither they, the Imperial Work Force nor the Italians were to be directly involved in the escape. One Japanese officer was to be killed and one wounded that night by stray bullets.

While the plan was being evolved, the sick and the lame were taking themselves off to quiet places where, without fuss, they selected their own suicides, traditional harakiri or the less-dramatic hanging. For the fit, a more extravagant end had been arranged. The final gesture comprised four simultaneous attacks, each of between 200-300 men. The first was the most risky, and was allocated to the occupants of the four huts to the north of the camp. Their mission was to seize the presently-unmanned, trailer-mounted No.2 Vickers gun situated at the northern end of the camp, before it could be reached by its crew; essentially a race against time. The stakes were worth the risks because, in Japanese hands, the machine-gun could be turned on to, and annihilate, B Company as they struggled from their accommodation to their stand-to positions.

The occupants in the remaining six huts closest to the outer perimeter fence, were instructed to force the wire opposite their huts. Their mission was to break clear into the open country and make rendezvous to the north of the camp, as a preliminary to forming the main assault group on the Recruit Training Unit. Of the remainder, those who occupied the inner line of huts, they were divided into two attack groups with separate axes once they had broken into Broadway. It was the intention that one group should turn north to storm the main gates, while the other group turned south in the direction of their officers' compound.

The prisoners waited patiently in their huts. Some drank their own potato-peel home-brew, as much to pass the time as to steel their nerves. It was not uncommon, in the traditions of the Japanese military, for their warriors to go into battle a little tiddly. The last farewells were made, and final preparations attended to. The fires were primed, and Minami was handed an English trumpet to sound the signal for the final Banzai. H-Hour was 2 am, when it was hoped that their guards, anaesthetised by the local brew, would be in deep slumber.

On the eve of the Cowra break-out, the Australian military strength comprised 39 officers and 607 other ranks. Among that number were 1 officer and 39 other ranks from 16 Australian Garrison Battalion, who had arrived from Hay along the small, serpentine railway, to act as escort for those Japanese due to leave Cowra on 7 August.

As forecast, it was a bright, crisp moonlit night. The singing and jollifications from the Italian compounds had now died down. The lights in the huts were out and the security lights bathed the key routes and fences in their artificial glow. As the bewitching hour passed, it was left to the sentries of the recently-instituted Broadway guard to reflect upon their misfortune. Cowra was an unpopular posting in much the same way as Darwin had been. The garrison unit did not have the youthful vitality, camaraderie and kind of excitement that can be generated in a unit with a combat role. For the guards, the weekends were a welcome oasis, a respite from the tedium and monotony of their routine. The addition of the Broadway guard to the roster merely extended each and every soldier's liability to the increased frequency of the regular and boring duties.

An eerie quiet prevailed throughout the camp. The solitary Broadway sentry sat inside his tent huddled in his greatcoat, cold but alert. On the two metre table in front of him was a field telephone which connected him to the Guard Commander in D Compound's guardroom. He had been warned to be particularly observant of the Japanese in B Compound and was reminded of the warning procedure to be followed in the event of an incident. It was at 1.45 am that the sentry's attention was caught by movement in the shadows between the huts. A Japanese soldier had broken under the strain. He wanted to live and was one of the minority who saw the utter futility in the Kanazawa plan. The man's identity was never discovered, but it was clear from his furtive actions that in endeavouring to communicate with the authorities he was at great pains to avoid being seen by his comrades in what they would regard as a traitorous act.

As the man stole from the huts towards the inner fence, he was spotted by a fellow-prisoner. Oblivious of his detection, the man used his blanket to good effect to scale the first fence. Once over, still carrying the blanket, now flapping from his hands held over his head, he made directly for the outer gate leading to Broadway. All the while, the terrified little man, weeping uncontrollably, shouted in a strained, shrill voice, warnings in Japanese punctuated by occasional indistinct words in English.

With the vociferous apparition making his determined progress towards the lone sentry, the Digger raised the muzzle of his .303 rifle in the air and squeezed the trigger twice. Almost immediately, the telephone in front of him rang. The sentry informed his Guard Commander of the voluble little Japanese whom he could not understand, but who appeared to be in fear of his life. He was ordered to pacify the prisoner and was promised an escort.

The fellow-prisoner who had witnessed the movements of the informer towards the fence, rushed in to report the occurrence to Minami. 'Get him!', screamed the airman. It was still ten minutes to H-Hour but, aware that the element of surprise was slipping away, Minami grabbed the trumpet. He threw open the door of Hut 13, admitting the icy air, and then blew the call to start the attack.

Meanwhile, in Broadway, the sentry was patiently awaiting assistance as he tried to reassure his excitable Japanese. It was not long before the two-man escort was to be seen jogging from B Company while, from the opposite direction of D Compound, an officer was making his way in the sentry's direction. When all four had made rendezvous, they could not make head nor tail of what the chattering prisoner was trying to communicate. It was at this point that the strident sound of the trumpet rose above the huts in B Compound. This seemed to excite the prisoner even more. His English vocabulary exhausted itself as the random, unintelligible utterance, 'strike-come-calaboose', sought desperately to convey to the Australians the peril they all faced, standing as they were in the middle of Broadway.

The noise of the commotion from B Compound suddenly dawned upon the officer as he turned towards the sound of the screamed banzais, to be confronted by a flood of red-uniformed prisoners flowing over or under the fences. Blankets were thrown over the wire or, in other cases, prisoners wrapped in blankets or greatcoats lay on the wire while their colleagues clambered over the top of them.

'Run for your lives', the officer ordered. They dashed the 50 metres to the gate at the southern end of Broadway. There was no supporting fire from the tower above them. Instead, one of the Broadway sentries turned, while the others passed through the gate, and shot the leader of the mob. He then retired hurriedly behind the gate, which was banged shut and secured. The unfortunate informer was left to his fate inside the compound. He ran, dodged, like a cornered hind, until overwhelmed by his avenging comrades. The wave's momentum did not pause as, seemingly in one movement, the man was kicked, clubbed and had his throat cut. The body was then tossed aside like a rag doll as the escape effort made its inexorable forward progress.

> The prisoners carried as weapons baseball bats, staves, improvised clubs and dining and kitchen knives which had been sharpened and some of which had also been serrated or pointed. Extra clothing was worn and the prisoners had towels wrapped around themselves. For protection against the entanglements and as protection for the hands, some wore baseball gloves, or specially prepared gloves made from the uppers of boots, while others wore pads of toilet paper.*

As the prisoners left their accommodation huts for the last time, they overturned the heating braziers. Upon the hot coke which had spewed out on to the floor, they flung the straw from their palliasses and other combustible materials. The full effect of the fires was slow to develop, but eventually the conflagration in B Compound was very evident, providing additional illumination of the Broadway activities as well as of the two separate attempts to negotiate the outer perimeter wire. Eighteen accommodation huts and two administration buildings were destroyed. Among the charred embers were the

---

* The Army Report

human remains of the incapacitated and the infirm, some 20 of those who could not, or would not, join the escape.

The general alarm was raised at approximately 01.50. At about that time, three red flares arched into the sky to warn the Recruit Training Unit but, to be certain, a telephone call was made to their Duty Officer. In the Australian accommodation huts, the Diggers had been alerted by the two rifle shots and a number were already turning out of their billets into the cold air, their greatcoats over the issued blue-striped pyjamas.

There is little doubt that both sides regarded the recently-arrived Vickers machine-guns as being the key weapons which, if in Australian hands, would go a long way towards stemming the outflow from the camp. If the weapons fell into Japanese hands, however, there was the promise of considerable loss of life among the Cowra garrison, not to mention a massive Japanese propaganda coup. The No.1 machine-gun was mounted below B Tower, to the east of the Broadway gates. The more vulnerable, trailer-mounted No.2 gun was sited 50 metres away from the Australian accommodation huts, in such a manner as to fire in a south-easterly direction towards F Tower.

The two rifle shots coincided with the start of the Japanese handicap race to take-over the unmanned No.2 machine-gun. They had to cover a greater distance than the gun's crew, and had the not inconsiderable disadvantage of a series of three barbed-wire obstacles to traverse. When Privates Ben Hardy and Ralph Jones, the gun crew, were shaken from their slumber they were quite naturally in their beds. The Japanese had already begun the 250 metre dash to the first fence.

The race was won by the two Diggers. Hardy, breathing heavily, squatted behind the gun in the Number One position, while Jones opened the frost-covered ammunition boxes to feed the first belt into the gun. There was no attempt to fire warning shots in this sector as Hardy engaged the proliferation of targets now over the first fence and negotiating the second. The Japanese fitness-training was being put to good use. It was at this stage that the camp's lighting failed, due in all probability to the overhead cables being severed by machine-gun fire. The absence of electric light posed no immediate problem to Hardy and Jones. There was a beneficial full-moon and, in addition, the blazing huts provided a fiery backdrop, silhouetting the Japanese targets on and around the wire.

It was not to be long before all three fences were cushioned by blankets and the bodies of those, the first to arrive, but who had died in their attempts to negotiate the wire. Still the machine-gun continued its death-dealing chatter, while the prisoners swarmed over the three fences as though at an Aintree Grand National. The wounded, caught and fixed to the wire, killed themselves with the knives they carried, or asked their colleagues following-on to end their lives. Their friends obliged.

With their weapons held firmly in their hands, the leaders were soon clear of the wire obstacles and scampered the 60 metres towards the red-hot gun, spewing death from its trailer but now unable to cope with the array of targets. The gun crew must have wondered in their last few minutes of life what had happened to the supporting fire that they had every right to expect. They were isolated, and surrounded by the fanatical prisoners clambering under, around and over the trailer. Hardy would have recognised that they were doomed, and told his mate Jones to make his escape. Jones dived over the heads of the encircling Japanese, but already the unforgiving clubs and knives were rising and falling. He dragged his battered and bludgeoned body to B Company lines where he died.

Meanwhile, on the trailer, Hardy was being rendered to pulp as a frenzied attack of clubs and knives rained down upon the lifeless body. What was left of Hardy was then unceremoniously thrown off the trailer to leave the way clear for the operation of the prized machine-gun. The Japanese were, of course, not familiar with the machine-gun now in their possession. They had studied it, however, from their side of the wire, and it did not take too long to fathom. The barrel was swung round to the west, the gun reloaded, and aim taken on the B Company lines. The trigger was squeezed, but the gun refused to come to life. Hardy's last mortal act had been to remove the gun's breechblock.

Now at long last, the Japanese who had swarmed over the trailer became subject to the slow-to-develop Australian counter-moves as a Lewis gun fired from the direction of the eastern end of B Company's huts. Prisoners were still clambering over the fences and, in order that the gun might not be used against them, the Japanese swung the inoperative gun through 180 degrees and locked it firmly before escaping into the night.

The guards soon resumed possession of the machine-gun and were able to bring it into action. The breech lock was found on the trailer floor among the ammunition belts. For their heroic, unsupported action, which had undoubtedly saved many Australian lives that night, 45 year old Private Ben Hardy and 43 year old Ralph Jones were recommended for a high gallantry award. The promulgation of the award of a suitable medal did not occur until six years later when, on 1 September 1950, King George VI approved the award to both dead soldiers, of the nation's highest non-operational bravery award – the George Cross.

The second group of escapees, those ordered to cross the perimeter wire near F Tower with a view to attacking the Recruit Training Unit, had an easier passage. The majority of the 334 who were able to make the clean break, escaped in this sector. The one sentry in F Tower who had unimpeded observation of the break-out below him, was barely effective. His Owen gun had but five clips of ammunition. In addition, he had his personal rifle and some grenades. There was no room in the cramped tower to throw the grenades and, since the Japanese were too far distant, their escape attempt was largely uninterrupted. The sentry soon exhausted his ammunition and, when he telephoned for more, he was told that there was no way of getting a re-supply to him. In contrast to the area in front of Hardy's gun, where over 50 bodies were festooned on the wire or lying lifeless on the ground, only five prisoners were killed in this, the second break-out across the perimeter fence.

The confusion in and around the camp was, for both sides, complete. The respective commanders were unable to exercise co-ordinated control over events developing on both sides of the wire, which had now devolved into quite separate side-shows. Kanazawa recognised that there was no point in his remaining in the self-styled command-post he had established in one of the huts, since there was nothing to command. He bade farewell to his deputy and crossed the wire near the No.2 machine-gun, disappearing up the hill. The air all around was heavy with the sound of whining bullets as junior commanders on the ground used their own initiiative to deal with the threat facing them. Whereas each company had individual contingency plans, the poor co-ordination between companies was evident. Three Australian soldiers fell to the ground with bullet wounds, even though at that stage the Japanese had been unable to get their hands on any weapons.

The Battalion's poor response and reaction to the emergency cannot be better exemplified than in the case of the performance of the No.1 machine-gun. It should be remembered that this particular Friday night was one of only three remaining over which serious trouble was perceived to be probable. The No.1 gun was only metres from the accommodation buildings, closer than Hardy's had been.

As has already been explained, it provided no supporting fire to Hardy's gun, not coming into action until after the No.2 machine-gun had been captured. The gun was eventually brought in to use by the Number Two, firing into the closely-packed Japanese ranks in front of Broadway's northern gates. Only later was the gunner joined by the gun's Number One.

The plight of that half of the prisoners nominated for the two divergent attacks along Broadway had now become serious. Even though the No.1 Vickers had only 1,000 rounds, it opened fire at a crucial time, when the developing swell of red-uniformed would-be escapees was building its momentum. That momentum was to be broken down and then destroyed by the scything effect of machine-gun bullets sending prisoners to ground to seek shelter in the storm drains along either side of Broadway.

The progress of those prisoners who had turned southward in the direction of their officers' compound had fared no better. The officers and men of the Battalion's D Company had been turned out, lining the wire in fire positions with their weapons pointing into the camp. A group of some 200 prisoners had now assembled outside the southern gates. They milled around in what was to be the lull before the storm. The Bren guns in the towers above them were uncertain and slow to open fire, but when they did, the soldiers along the wire joined in, causing the Japanese to disperse rapidly. A few took to the ditches, where they were to remain while a knot of 50 prisoners surged towards the officers' compound, taking the double gates with them. Many prisoners lay dead in front of the Broadway gates and on the ground in D Compound. Those who survived the onslaught of fire, desperately sought shelter in the ditches and behind the huts, having apparently abandoned the mission's whole *raison d'être* – their own human sacrifice.

The risk of an outbreak from either end of Broadway had been nipped in the bud. Sporadic sorties were launched against the northern gates but, in the main, the prisoners had gone to ground. To move, invited a bullet from eager guards with scores to settle. For those prisoners who had reassessed their personal situation, the best they could do was to hug the frosty ground in ditches, drains, indentations or behind huts and await the dawn.

In the last hour of darkness, therefore, the situation had been reached where the only successful escape attempts had been made over the perimeter fence near F Tower and, to a lesser degree, in front of the No.2 machine-gun. Most of the escapees assembled among the rocks and trees on the high ground overlooking the blazing B Compound. Some infiltrated through the hospital, staff accommodation and administrative buildings. An attempt was made on the life of Major Ramsay, frustrated only by a soldier discharging his rifle at almost point-blank range at the knife-wielding assassin. One 31-year old Australian soldier did die here, said to have been fatally stabbed in the heart. Unsubstantiated rumours persisted, that he was in fact killed by an Australian bullet, a victim of the wild, random and unco-ordinated fire which was such a feature that night.

A patrol of one officer and 16 men was despatched to the Soil Conservation Station (still there), after reports of an accumulation of prisoners in the vicinity. The action around the rocks, trees and long grass was confused, but the patrol's presence served to disperse the prisoners. The majority headed north, but one group of approximately 40 drifted towards the town and the direction of the Recruit Training Unit. This group showed no great sense of purpose, nor intent to carry out their mission – to raid the Recruit Unit. Whereas they had succeeded in breaking out, they had been unable to secure the weapons with which to attack the by-now fully-alerted training battalions. As they dallied, they were intercepted by half-a-dozen soldiers from the prison who had no great difficulty, after reinforcement, in shepherding the reluctant assault troops back towards their compound. All the mopping-up action was conducted by the prison's battalion. It was not until mid-afternoon that the staff and soldiers of the Recruit Battalions were mobilised to scour the countryside for those escapees still at large.

The desultory patrolling in the region of the Soil Conservation Station continued. A rifle was lost, then regained, while a number of prisoners, sensing their failure, indulged in selective suicides. One or two hanged themselves from the kurrajong trees, while others attempted harakiri or simply cut their throats with their kitchen knives. An Australian soldier received stab wounds in the neck and shoulder after one encounter. Daylight would reveal a dozen scattered, wounded Japanese as well as the dead, several with knives still tightly clutched in their rigid hands.

Inside the camp, the ditches and drains were filled with those who had survived as well as the dead and the dying. Eighteen metres from the officers' compound was the body of Tadao Minami. He had been struck down by the burst of Bren-fire from the towers and fell into a ditch, severely wounded. He took from his pocket a last cigarette which he lit, and puffed, before putting down. He then picked up a carving-knife and cut through his jugular. In that cut, the Japanese lost their real leader. There were now no recognised leaders inside the compound. Kanazawa had hobbled off over the hills, leaving his deputy in charge. The deputy's lifeless body was now in a nearby hut, dangling from a rope hanging from the rafters.

When Lieutenant-Colonel Brown rang Victoria Barracks, Sydney at 2.40 am, he was able to provide only the barest outline of what had happened. In military parlance, it was not dissimilar to a Contact Report which promises more to come with the phrase, 'Wait Out'. All that Brown could report at this early stage was that the break-out from B Compound had occurred, and that measures were in-hand to round-up the escapees. He returned to his duties to regain control of the situation and gather the statistics which his professional intuition told him would urgently be demanded. The news he passed to Sydney rattled through the political and military corridors like a dose of dysentery.

The initial reaction of the Adjutant-General was to order a news blackout on the escape. His ruling was to be challenged by his own public relations men, who pointed out that the imposition of a blanket censorship would mean that the civilians living in and around Cowra could not be warned of the danger that they were assumed to be facing. The threat was a not-unreasonable assumption, for the authorities could not have been aware that prior to the break-out, Kanazawa had ordered his men not to harm civilians. That order was meticulously observed. The General thereupon reconsidered his instructions, agreeing that the public should be notified but with the caveat that there was to be no reference to Japanese, the numbers involved, or details of casualties.

The news of the break-out was given on the early-morning ABC News. All that the public was able to discover was that a number of prisoners of undisclosed nationality had broken out of the Cowra internment camp. The listeners were reassuringly advised that the area was being searched by the police and military. They were warned not to assist the prisoners, but were to report any requests for help directly to the authorities. That same, bald information was released to the press with supporting reporting restrictions. The brevity of the statement prompted national and international war correspondents with noses for stories, to look up Cowra on the map and be on their way before the early-morning sun had climbed very high in the sky.

The Adjutant-General would issue no further instructions on censorship, a matter taken under the wing of the Federal Ministry of

Information before it was to receive Prime Minister Curtin's personal attention. The District Headquarters did, however, announce on Sunday that all the prisoners had been 'accounted for', even though it was known that a hardcore of determined prisoners was still at large. As a result of this intended deception, the by-now very tired civilian police were obliged to tour the countryside informing people not to relax their vigilance.

* * *

The censorship issue which had been so evident at Darwin and Broome had festered-on between the press and the Government. Editors have a group-consciousness to report matters of public interest which just happen to have a tendency to be synonymous with increased circulation and profits. They regarded the Ministry of Information in general, and Minister Arthur Calwell in particular, as being over-zealous in their policing of the censorship laws, and suspected the reason was to do with political expediency. Matters came to a head during Easter 1944. Newspapers were seized, leading to that action being tested in the High Court. The judges ruled that newspapers were free to publish articles on the subject of censorship. This had been a limited judgement, and did not provide editors with *cartes blanches* to publish matters which the Chief Censor ruled should not be published in the national interest.

Throughout the weekend, efforts at political and military damage-control had moved on apace. General Sir Thomas Blamey, the Commander-in-Chief of the Australian Military Forces, had communicated to the Prime Minister a recommended outline of their response to the outbreak. Curtin had, of course, been an information addressee to the Featherstone correspondence which had passed between the New Zealand and British governments. He remained extremely sensitive lest the news of the outbreak, and details of what was developing to be an alarmingly high casualty list, should be released prematurely to the Japanese Government. The fear of reprisals to Australian and Allied prisoners-of-war was uppermost in his mind. Already, Blamey had ordered a Court of Inquiry to be convened, to meet at Cowra on Monday 7 August, and urged the Prime Minister to maintain strict censorship until the findings of the inquiry were released. Blamey must have been confident from his briefings by the Adjutant-General, that nothing prejudicial or blameworthy would arise from what was essentially an in-house military inquiry. The Commander-in-Chief recommended to his Prime

Minister that the findings of the Inquiry should be the basis of the initial communication to the Japanese through the usual offices of the Swiss intermediaries.

Efforts to keep the lid on the matter until the appropriate time, were dashed with the publication of the *Sunday Telegraph*. Both Curtin and Blamey were horrified to read in the headline article, the details of the break-out and the broadest hint possible that the prisoners involved were Japanese. The Government cast its net wide in an attempt to plug the leak, even going so far as to request that Britain use her good offices with the Swiss to prevent details of the break-out reaching the Japanese before the Inquiry's findings were to hand. The Swiss had been too quick-off-the-mark, passing on to the Japanese Government the bare, available information concerning the escape. Curtin, who was now handling the censorship issue personally rather than through his discredited Minister Calwell, wrote a stern letter to the editor of the *Sunday Telegraph*, demanding an apology. There is no record of any apology being forthcoming.

* * *

First light on Saturday morning revealed to the camp authorities the first inkling of the size of the disaster. All but three of the accommodation huts in B Compound were smouldering ruins, three areas of wire were draped heavily with hundreds of blankets and tens of bodies, but the majority of the now-bewildered prisoners had responded to the ceasefire. Those who tested the authorities in final acts of bravado were shot.

Major Ramsay had been quick to call in supplementary troops from the Recruit Training Unit to reinforce his hard-pressed company. The reserves from the other companies in the prison's battalion were engaged on local patrol duties. There was still no attempt to call out the Training Unit's other stand-by troops to assist in a wider search for the escapees. Thirteen hours would elapse before they were invited to assist. For the moment, however, Lieutenant-Colonel Brown's most pressing requirement was to organise the treatment of the wounded and collection of the dead. A medical team was cobbled together from within the Cowra Garrison and the immediate vicinity, to repair injuries which even the most experienced of surgeons had rarely seen; gunshot wounds, botched disembowellings, and throats torn at by rudimentary instruments.

A mid-day headcount on Saturday told the camp authorities who was in and who was out. They were still unable to finalise the casualty list. That the camp staff were unused to continuous operations or the taxing effect of fear and excitement upon their energies, was reflected in a general and obvious state of fatigue. The staff were aware that 378 prisoners were unaccounted for, and that the responsibility for their apprehension would, for the main part, now have to rest on the reserves waiting in the nearby Recruit Training Unit.

The call-out of the reserve troops to join the search was not made until 3.30 pm on Saturday, by which time the prisoners were well-dispersed. It was just before last light that the convoy drove out of the gates of the Recruit Training Unit and took the road north towards Canowindra.* On board were 23 officers and 588 men. The vast majority of the 'men' comprised partly-trained or untrained and frightened boys, no more than 18 years old. The reputation of the Japanese as cunning, brave and skilful fighters was quite naturally well-known to their worried hunters. The group's orders were to drive ten kilometres north of the prisoner-of-war camp, and then to conduct a sweep southward between the Canowindra and Binni Creek roads as far as the prison camp. All prisoners were to be captured alive. Furthermore, so strong was the fear of reprisals, and the marksmanship of the recruits so uncertain, that the entire search party had nothing for their own personal protection but bayonets. Even the veteran instructors were forbidden to carry arms, a decision which must have galled marksman Lieutenant Harry Doncaster. He would have been aware that, if any Japanese were intercepted, they were sure to fight in the hope of inflicting casualties on their Australian hunters. They had, after all, no prospect of joining up with their own forces.

When Doncaster's platoon de-bussed, it was already becoming dark, and a cold but gentle breeze was stirring the branches of the kurrajong trees. The light from the moon made its presence felt, reflecting from the boulders and trees, casting dark shadows on the feature to their immediate front. It was decidedly eerie. 'Follow me', ordered Doncaster, as he led his reluctant heroes up the gentle slope towards the uncertainties in the darkness. As the platoon commander passed between the rocks near the summit, he was pounced upon by a group of prisoners, and killed. The remainder of the platoon fled in terror.

Soon, an armed platoon of experienced soldiers arrived from the camp, in response to the insistent demands of one of the senior offi-

---

* Pronounced *Canowndra*.

cers out there on the ground. He had already determined that they had been sent out on a fool's errand, searching unarmed for desperate men. They retraced the steps that Doncaster had taken and, at 10.30 pm, found his body lying face down. He had been stabbed in the back and his head had been smashed in. A search of the immediate area revealed the bodies of what were assumed to have been his assailants, six hanging from the branches of the kurrajong and two at the foot of the trees.

A larger, follow-up armed patrol found more bodies that night and gradually, dead or alive, the audit of the escapees continued. The fragility of the situation and continuing need for secrecy was further impaired on Sunday when an off-duty railway worker killed two prisoners with his shotgun. Censorship took on a new dimension, for civilians are less susceptible to gagging than the military. On the railway itself, two further prisoners had placed their necks on the line in front of the local train. Their headless bodies were taken back to the camp's open-air mortuary to join the accumulating pile of those who were either killed or who had taken their own lives. In total, 25 bodies of escapees were added to those killed in or within the camp surrounds. The business of identification, categorisation of cause of death, and documentation, was underway, being conducted by the War Graves Service and representatives of the Coroner's Court.

The interception, recapture and collection of prisoners went on for nine days – long after the Army had implied that all escapees had been captured. The round-up was enthusiastically supported by the local community, unknowingly immune to Japanese violence. Among the 334 recaptured was Sergeant-Major Kanazawa who, like so many of his colleagues, had somehow failed in his pact with death.

* * *

The members of the Court of Inquiry convened to investigate the occurrences at the camp, assembled at Cowra on Monday 7 August. At that time, there were still prisoners at large, the hospitals were full of casualties, the dead were barely identified, let alone buried, and the killing had not yet ended. It was quite evident that a quick, exonerating report was hoped for from what was a surprisingly low-ranking committee of one Colonel, one Lieutenant-Colonel and two Majors. The Prime Minister and General Blamey were waiting. The terms of reference given to the members of the Inquiry were to inquire into, and report on, the circumstances surrounding the incident and all matters and facts related to, or in any way connected with it, and the conduct of any person or persons in relation thereto. With time of the essence, the general trend of the investigation was to concentrate almost exclusively on what had happened, rather than why it had happened.

The members of the Inquiry spent their first day on orientation. They toured B Compound, examined the fences, visited the camp hospital, and inspected the dead. That night, the first batch of identified corpses, wrapped in red blankets, was trucked surreptitiously down to the Japanese section of the nearby war cemetery. There, in the heavily-piqueted burial ground, a bulldozer gouged out the resting places for the red bundles. Australian soldiers, assisted by Italian prisoners, worked quietly and reverently by the light of lanterns, placing the bodies as indicated by the officers of the Graves Registration Service.

The Inquiry came to order after lunch on Tuesday, proceeding for one week to take the evidence of 61 witnesses in camera. Among that number were seven Japanese.

The behaviour of the 12 Japanese officers is worthy of examination. After the break-out, five of them sent a petition to the authorities, admitting that they too had been implicated, and demanding to be shot as a punishment. The spontaneity of the uprising was such that there had been no time for the NCOs to co-ordinate the activities of their officers, nor to involve them in the plot. This had, therefore, left the officers in an invidious position. They feared that if reports were misinterpreted in Japan, it might appear that they had abstained from joining the insurrection.

A brief, written on lavatory paper, was smuggled across from the officers' compound to Kanazawa, now languishing in B Compound's detention cage. The note suggested to the NCO the reasons for his course of action, why the men escaped, the crossing of the wire, and the burning of the huts. Overall, however, he was prompted to emphasise that the primary cause for the break-out had been the strong Japanese opposition to the segregation of NCOs and other-ranks. The officers even went so far as to suggest to Kanazawa the reason why they, the officers, had not been consulted. It was simply that Kanazawa had felt that the stage had been reached where further discussion was pointless. With a strong hint of self-preservation in evidence, the officers stressed that Kanazawa should insist that the decision to break-out was spontaneous, and not preconceived.

Kanazawa was to be the Inquiry's penultimate witness. He provided a written statement, supplemented by a verbal report to the Inquiry.

He kept loyally to the brief provided by his officers, a fact that could be verified by Australian Intelligence who had found the note in Kanazawa's possession. He stressed that the incident had been initiated by the decision to segregate NCOs and other-ranks. He felt that the extreme reaction of the Japanese might well have been avoided had some explanation as to the justification been forthcoming.

Two Japanese officers also gave evidence before the Inquiry. Notwithstanding their arrogant and demanding demeanor, their question begged a studied answer in view of the evidence that had gone before. How was it possible, they asked, that one of their officers had been killed and another wounded? The senior Japanese officer insisted that the question be investigated. It never was. It was put in the 'too difficult' category, an unwelcome complication. After all, a key question which the Inquiry had to examine was the use of minimum force, and confirmation that fire had been stringently controlled. Major Ramsay had already advised the Inquiry that fire had been controlled. He was not cross-examined as to how two Japanese officers not involved in the escape attempt had been shot, nor the manner in which three of his own soldiers had been wounded by their own comrades. The Inquiry recorded that fire was only directed at escapees or those threatening the guards, and that it was stopped as soon as was practicable, avoiding unnecessary casualties.

After taking evidence for a week, the Inquiry moved to Sydney to consider its findings. All those Australians directly involved in the incident had been interviewed, and provision had also been made to take the evidence of those Japanese who had expressed a desire to appear before the Court. The findings and record of proceedings of the Inquiry were a relief to the Prime Minister or General Blamey. In sumary, they were:

1. The use of arms was stopped at the earliest possible moment having regard to the circumstances.

2. The discipline and general conduct of the guards was highly satisfactory and there was no evidence of any wrongful acts or omissions toward the prisoners-of-war or of the illegitimate use of force during the recapture of escapees by AMF patrols.

3. The mass escape and attack was carried out according to a premeditated and concerted plan but there had been no opportunity to convey details to the Japanese officers in D Compound.

4. The objective was to overthrow the security of the Group and to sell their own lives in suicidal combat.

5. The arrangements for medical attention and treatment of casualties were satisfactory.

6. All possible care was taken in the identification of bodies and the dead were buried with all due respect and reverence in the War Cemetery at Cowra.

The Inquiry's findings were then subjected to so much high-level examination and tinkering, that Prime Minister Curtin's report of the incident was not available for release until one month after the event. It was the stuff of which the bureaucrat dreams. The great irony, however, was that the meticulous attention to detail and covering of all bases, was to prove to be absolutely unnecessary. It is, however, difficult to fault the Curtin Government's honourable motives.

Featherstone camp had been established by New Zealand in response to a request from the United States to take a proportion of the unexpectedly large number of prisoners arising from the Guadalcanal operations. At the same time, a significant number of prisoners were assigned to Cowra and, like those shot in New Zealand, they were therefore the responsibility of the United States. Of the Cowra dead, 118 were judged to have been held on behalf of the United States Government. Accordingly, America along with Britain had to be drawn into the long consultative process.

All kinds of provisos and considerations were raised by the enlarged but dispersed Committee. Actions and reactions likely to arise from both sides were methodically weighed and assessed. There was concern as to the reaction of the largely autonomous Japanese military leaders on the periphery of the Greater East Asia Co-Prosperity Sphere. For example, those in Singapore and Batavia held large numbers of Australian and Allied prisoners-of-war. It was thought essential that they should be prevented from exercising their delegated military powers until Tokyo had issued guidelines after what was hoped would be rational political consideration. It was all a matter of timing. For that reason, it was decided that the Prime Minister's statement would be released simultaneously at home and abroad. In that way, it was hoped that local Japanese commanders would be dissuaded from a spontaneous military response by being forewarned to await political guidance from Tokyo.

On 2 September, the agreed initial document began its journey to Berne via the Swiss Consul-General in Sydney. It was a bland, defensive report which raised as many questions as it answered. It even gave tacit support to the Japanese prisoners' stand against segregation.

After discussion, a decision was made that there was to be no hint in the report of the segregation issue. The justification was on the grounds that the application of segregation upon Allied prisoners-of-war would deprive the junior ranks of support considered to be vital to their prospects of surviving their captivity.

A week was allowed to elapse for the transit of the document before Curtin made his public announcement on 9 September. The statement was based on the findings of the Court of Inquiry. Doubtless the Australian public were gratified to hear that their own soldiers had demonstrated great discipline and restraint, and relieved to hear that, 'the onus for the incident rests entirely upon the prisoners-of-war themselves'. Meanwhile, Intelligence and Signals intercept were on full alert to discover the Axis powers' reaction. Berlin's response was immediate, coming on the same day that Curtin made his announcement. The content of the report was predictable, decrying what it described as a breach of accepted rules of behaviour. For the first Japanese reaction, however, the authorities would have to wait another day.

A Batavia radio news item was intercepted by Signals Intelligence. The report contained an unexpected twist, confirming that the Japanese Government was not prepared, under any circumstances, to acknowledge the possibility of the existence of Japanese prisoners-of-war. It was argued that, since the 200 'innocent' Japanese who were murdered could not have been servicemen, they must have been civilians such as those who had been interned from Darwin and Broome!

> It is perfectly clear to the Japanese people that these poor unfortunate Japanese who were murdered in the prison camp cannot have been prisoners-of-war for it is a well known and accepted fact that the Japanese soldier never permits himself to be taken prisoner. His military creed is that death by his own hand is preferable to the dishonour and humiliation of capture by the enemy. Curtin may not care to admit it, but the fact then is perfectly obvious that the unfortunate victims of the midnight mass murder were internees who had lived in Australia long years before the war.

In time, when the full document with supporting appendices and nominal rolls reached Tokyo, it was obvious that those who had been killed at Cowra were indisputably prisoners-of-war. Even if she felt inclined to derive political capital from the results of the break-out, Japan would have to weigh such benefit against the dilution of the Military Code. At no time in the war had it been more imperative for servicemen to make their ultimate sacrifice for Nippon. This was not the time to publicise and condone surrender. What the prisoners of Cowra had made therefore, had been a pointless gesture. The loss of 231 Japanese servicemen killed and 108 wounded was never to become a propaganda issue. It was a subject about which Tokyo neither wanted to know, nor cared.

* * *

A relieved Australian Government set about the final administration of the affair, tying up loose ends before the whole matter was put under wraps and, until recently, largely forgotten. The need for a civilian coroner's inquiry was not disputed, but its progress, even in camera, was marked by obstruction, prevarication and over-zealous control. Kanazawa was brought to trial for murder and for a secondary, minor charge. He was found 'not guilty' of murder, but guilty of the minor offence, for which he was awarded 19 months' hard labour. Within the camp, the prisoners had not dismissed the prospect of a repetition of the events of 5 August. The auth-orities, however, were never to provide them with a suitable oppor-tunity. Major Ramsay retired soon after the event and, although exonerated of all blame by the Inquiry, Lieutenant-Colonel Brown went the same way as Darwin's Wing-Commander Griffith – relieved of his command.

* * *

A great deal had gone wrong at Cowra, in much the same way as had gone wrong at Darwin and Broome. It had been a most undistinguished military performance that became submerged in thankful secrecy. Any student of history going to Cowra today to find a musuem or display which outlines the details of the happenings that morning of 5 August 1944, will be disappointed. No such record exists. It is as though the community has erased the past from its mind, preferring instead to take the path of reconciliation. That atti-tude is exemplified in Cowra's showpiece, the tranquil environment of the Japanese Garden and Cultural Centre, opened on 21 October 1979 by Mr Shigeo Nagano, President of the Japanese Chamber of Commerce and Industry.

Epilogue

Cemeteries have been a sad feature of this trilogy. There was the poignant, moving atmosphere of the Adelaide River Commonwealth War Cemetery, the last resting-place of the Darwin victims. Broome had its irregular, historical Japanese cemetery, but that at Cowra is strangely serene and symbolic. Until 1963, maintenance of the Japanese War Cemetery had depended upon the goodwill and devotion of local individuals and the Returned Servicemen's League. In October 1963, in response to the obvious need to adopt a more formalised arrangement, the expansive lawns were officially ceded to Japan. It was to Cowra that the bodies of airmen killed on the north coast were brought, as well as the young and old who had died in internment. In total, an additional 275 bodies were brought in from outside Cowra to this, their last resting-place.

In 1964, the new cemetery was opened, financed by the Japanese Government. It is now included on the schedule of many Japanese visitors to Australia, but perhaps the most important and significant mourners were the Emperor and Empress of Japan who were then Crown Prince Akihito and Princess Nishiko. They were impressed by the beauty of the cemetery, which had been designed complete with traditional stone lantern, or *ishidoro*, by the Tokyo architect, Shigaru Yura. Flanking the lawns are the trees common to Australia, the wattle and the gum, but also a tree that flourishes in this area and one that would have been recognised by the dead warriors of Nippon, the flowering cherry. Set slightly proud in the manicured lawns are 522 identical, flat gravestones, of which 231 bear on their descriptive metal plates, 'Died on 5 August 1944'.

The middle section of the cemetery, which separates the Australians from the Japanese, had been the burial ground of those Italian prisoners who had died of natural causes while in captivity. Their remains were repatriated soon after the war ended. Only metres separate the graves of Lieutenant Harry Doncaster and the two winners of the GC, Privates Hardy and Jones from that of Tadao Minami and the 230 of his fellow prisoners who died on that fatal night. Now, in this quiet Australian cemetery, rest the total of those

Japanese servicemen who had made their way onto mainland Australia. Very few of those, of course, had been killed on or above the continent. They had come from other campaigns in other territories. That there had not been more was Australia's greatest fortune of the war.

Selected Bibliography

ABBOTT, C L A, *Australia's Frontier Province*, (Sydney, 1950).

ASADA, Teruhiko, *The Night of a Thousand Suicides*, (Sydney, 1970).

BENEDICT, Ruth, *The Chrysanthemum and the Sword*, (London, 1967).

BENNETT-BREMNER, E, *Front Line Airline*, (Sydney, 1944).

BROWN, David, *Carrier Operations in WWII*, (London, 1974).

CHURCHILL, Winston S, *The Second World War Vol. IV: The Hinge of Fate*, (London, 1951).

CLARKE, Hugh, *Break Out!*, (Sydney, 1965).

EDWARDS, Hugh, *Port of Pearls*, (Adelaide, 1983).

GORDON, Harry, *Die Like the Carp*, (Australia, 1978).

GRIFFITHS, Owen, *Darwin Drama*, (Sydney, 1946).

HALL, Timothy, *Darwin 1942*, (Australia, 1980).

HASLUCK, Paul, *The Government and the People 1939-41*, (Canberra, 1952).

ITO, Masanori, *The End of the Imperial Japanese Navy*, (London, 1962).

KENNEDY, Paul, *Pacific Onslaught*, (USA, 1972).

KEOGH, Colonel E G, *South West Pacific 1941-45*, (Melbourne, 1965)

LIVERPOOL, Lord Russell of, *The Knights of Bushido*, (London, 1958).

LOCKWOOD, Douglas, *Australia's Pearl Harbour*, (Sydney, 1966).

LONG, Gavin, *To Benghazi*, (Canberra, 1952).

LONG, Gavin, *The Final Campaigns*, (Canberra, 1963).

MacKENZIE, Kenneth, *Dead Men Rising*, (Sydney, 1969).

MANDLE, W F, *Going it Alone*, (Australia, 1978).

MEANEY, Neville K, *A History of Australian Defence and Foreign Policy*, (Sydney, 1976).

MILLAR, T. (Thomas) B, *Australia's Defence*, (Melbourne, 1969).

MILLAR, T. (Thomas) B, *Australia in Peace and War: External Relations 1788- 1977*, (Canberra, 1978).

POWELL, Alan, *The Shadow's Edge: Australia's Northern War*, (Melbourne, 1988).

PRIME, Mervyn W, *WA's Pearl Harbour*, (RAAF Association, Australia, undated).

SHUNSUKE, Tsurumi, *An Intellectual History of Wartime Japan 1931-45*, (London, 1986).

THOMAS, David, *Battle of the Java Sea*, (London, 1968).

THORNE, Christopher, *Allies of a Kind*, (London, 1978).

TYLER, W H, *Flight of Diamonds*, (Carlisle, WA, 1987).

WARD, Russel, *The History of Australia*, (London, 1978).

OFFICIAL SOURCES

The Brisbane Line (Australian Archives)

CA12 The Prime Minister's Department 1911-1971

    AS 27/1/1 Brisbane Line

    CRS A 463 Correspondence, files, annual single murder series

               1956-58/1228 Commission on the Brisbane Line

CA46 Department of Defence

    MP 1217   Records of Sir Frederick Shedden. Box 2231

                Brisbane Line, 1943-1955

Index

Index